Jeff Chen

BRIDGE
CROSSWORDS

Edited by Ray Lee

AN HONORS BOOK FROM MASTER POINT PRESS

Honors Books is an imprint of Master Point Press.

Master Point Press
331 Douglas Ave.
Toronto, Ontario, Canada
M5M 1H2
(416) 781-0351

Email
info@masterpointpress.com

Websites
www.masterpointpress.com
www.bridgeblogging.com
www.teachbridge.com
www.ebooksbridge.com

ISBN 978-1-55494-770-6

EDITOR'S INTRODUCTION

I've always been a puzzle fan, although I confess that I grew up in England with cryptic crosswords, which are still my first love. However, good cryptics are few and far between in Canada, and eventually I decided to try the *New York Times* crosswords. To my surprise, I found them not only enjoyable, but challenging, although very different from the ones I was used to. Soon the Friday, Saturday, Sunday puzzles became a regular feature of my week, and I began buying books of *New York Times* crosswords so I could take puzzles with me on long trips.

With this in my background, it was easy to say 'yes' when Jeff Chen approached me a few months ago and asked me whether we would be interested in publishing a book of bridge crosswords. It was also a chance for me to try something new — editing crosswords. Jeff's puzzles have appeared in the *New York Times* and the *Los Angeles Times*, and you will find, as I did, that he is an ingenious constructor with a good sense of humor. He has been a pleasure to work with, except for being inconsiderate enough to go on honeymoon just when we needed him to start checking proofs.

All the puzzles in this book have a bridge flavor, sometimes in unexpected ways. They range from Easy (about *New York Times* Monday level) to Challenging (about *New York Times* Thursday level). I hope you have as much fun solving them as Jeff and I did putting them together.

Ray Lee

SECTION 1:
EASY

Across

1. House of Havana
5. "Terrible" czar
9. Is behind
13. Burden
14. Farm storage tower
15. Charges off
17. Bad thing to be behind
19. A nephew of Donald Duck
20. Beehive State resident
21. Twirl, as with thumbs
23. Harder to find
24. Christmas tree, typically
26. Juicy tropical fruit
28. Ming of the NBA
29. Misbid, e.g.
31. Reader's Digest co-founder Wallace
33. Unusual bid, sometimes
37. Amigo
38. Topic of an old saw at the starts of 17-, 24-, 49-, and 59-across

40. Grand Life Master Mahmood
41. Large book size
43. Pluck
44. Coffeehouse music genre
45. Embrace
47. Immobile in winter
49. Cat's attribute, so it's said
53. At attention
56. Observant of Zero Tolerance, e.g.
57. Braying sound
58. Birch of "American Beauty"
59. Raven's cry
62. Delphic prophetess
63. Australian isl.
64. "Hard ___!" (helmsman's cry)
65. Bell sound
66. Red card, of a sort
67. Colorful salamander

Down

1. Heart of Le Havre
2. "West Side Story" girl
3. Placebo, sometimes
4. Pile of refuse
5. Amazon ID
6. Airline ticket word
7. Pledge of Allegiance closer
8. "The Prince of Tides" star
9. Commit morally or legally
10. Warren's predecessor
11. Avoid
12. Attendance counter
16. Caught in the act

18. Ball field covering
22. Crooked
24. Checking out
25. "Rhoda" star Harper
27. Clay, today
29. Cover letters?
30. ___-tzu
32. Converse competitor
34. Antarctic environmental concern
35. Nada
36. Common deciduous tree
38. It's not fair

What Are The Odds?

39. Abbr. for Jeanne d'Arc
42. "Right on!"
44. He goes to blazes
46. Jazz musician Evans
48. Big game?
49. D.C. ball team
50. "Gotcha, bro"
51. Weeper of myth
52. Lets off steam
54. 1970's batting champ Rod
55. Modern status update
57. Cord fiber
60. "Dig in!"
61. Brandy letters

Across

1. Irving protagonist
5. Q.E.D. word
9. Maori figurines
14. "Hold it right there!"
15. Fish also called blue jack
16. "Yes we can" sloganeer
17. Life story (abbr.)
18. Briefcase fastener
19. 1996 Madonna role
20. Giant lizards with deeply forked tongues
23. Digression of sorts
25. Like molasses
26. Native American ceremonial sauna
30. Single malt scotch brand
34. Today, in Tijuana
35. Take back, for short
36. Oral Roberts University site
37. Last name in horror
38. "The coast is clear!"
41. DSL purveyor
42. Esau's father
44. Sch. for youngsters
45. Big fat zero
46. Between, briefly
47. Mishmash
50. FBI figures
52. Part of TWA
53. Declarer play technique, and a hint to the circled letters
59. "A Room with ___"
60. Ellen DeGeneres's role in "Finding Nemo"
61. Marc Antony's love, for short
64. Temporary tattoo dye
65. Venomous "monster"
66. Fourth-best, often
67. Congregation members
68. Opening scene?
69. Orphaned Brontë heroine

Down

1. White house letters before 16-across
2. Sashimi serving
3. It's a first in baseball
4. Taiwanese temple
5. Trump ____ (count signal)
6. Main drag, e.g.
7. "I get it," facetiously
8. Head honcho
9. Translucent mineral
10. "Pretty please with a cherry on top?"
11. Big name in corn syrup
12. "That's my cue!"
13. Lacking, in Lyon
21. System adopted by much of the world
22. Pre-schoolers?
23. Fireplace receptacle
24. Nike's logo
27. Service infraction
28. Special ___
29. Gave, as an Rx
31. Dead end
32. Pass out
33. View from Vesuvius
36. Tantalizes
39. Math subj.

Turnabout is Fair Play

40. Overdue penalty
43. Enhance
47. Possessive pronoun
48. Keyed up
49. "The _____ of Omaha" (Warren Buffett)
51. Signature tune for Sinatra
53. "James and the Giant Peach" author Roald
54. Colored part of the eye
55. 2004 iPod debut
56. Hand feature sometimes shown with a splinter
57. Mystery writer ___ Stanley Gardner
58. All-time strikeout king
62. Musical aptitude, so to speak
63. Tribute in verse

Across

1. Taj Mahal locale
5. Own (up to)
9. Switch
14. Select from a deck
15. Go ballistic
16. Boxcar riders
17. Sixth letter of the Greek alphabet
18. Sock or switch ender
19. 51-across, e.g.
20. "Bridge is such a sensational game that I wouldn't mind being in jail if I had three cellmates who were decent players and who were willing to keep the game going 24 hours a day."
23. Ball belle, briefly
24. Guess at the best contract, e.g
25. Hits the jackpot
29. With lightness
34. One of the Gabors
35. Get ___ of reality
38. Brest friend
39. "Bridge is the most entertaining and intelligent card game the wit of man has so far devised."
43. Jurassic Park "star"
44. Give the cold shoulder
45. Dvorak's "Symphony No. 9 ___ Minor"
46. Big club, e.g.
49. Gaga
51. One was held in TN in 2012
54. Amorous murmur
55. "The best chess-player in Christendom may be little more than the best player of chess; but proficiency in whist (a forerunner to bridge) implies capacity for success in all those more important undertakings where mind struggles with mind."
61. "Git!"
62. Primary
63. A&W rival
65. It's a snap
66. Grackle, e.g.
67. Columbus' home
68. Big name in polls
69. "Not quite sure yet..."
70. Moxie

Down

1. Carpenter's curved cutter
2. Expanded
3. Pro ___
4. Mini-McKenneys, e.g.
5. Responses over competition, sometimes
6. Acquire, as masterpoints
7. Snooty sorts
8. Guinness, e.g.
9. Hoover's outfit
10. Wander
11. Lookout for, say
12. Convention used against 1NT openings
13. Bridge player in France?
21. Concrete-reinforcing rod

22. Air marshal's org.
25. A quarter of the seats at a 51-across
26. Scrimshaw's medium
27. When doubled, sings
28. Makes a move
30. Dust collector
31. Paintball cry
32. Hansen of public radio
33. Modern locale of ancient Sheba
36. Frequent race-car sponsor
37. Producers of green eggs
40. Business card abbr.
41. Hot date, in slang
42. Jack preceder
47. Beguile
48. Scuff up
50. Big enchiliada
52. Buck of filmdom
53. "I'll take the rest", e.g.
55. High-low, sometimes
56. Fall, like a stiff king
57. St. Peter's post
58. Euro predecessor
59. "Magnum P.I." setting
60. Abridge
61. Apr. Fools' season
64. Redouble's meaning, sometimes (abbr.)

ACROSS

1. Comic strip featuring Earl and Mooch
6. Breakfast chain acronym
10. Shoe with a "swoosh" logo
14. Bugged
15. Stellar blast
16. Seeing to the task
17. Place for odds and ends
19. Pro follower
20. Featured instrument of "Peter and the Wolf"
21. Bid 2NT in first seat, e.g.
22. Corrodes
23. The 4S of 1S-2S-3S-4S, e.g.
25. Bridge party thrower
26. Work like a dog
31. Billiards bounce
34. Scholarly book
35. Actress Zadora
36. Lose, as a lead
37. Pipsqueak
39. "Yan Can Cook" cookers
40. University URL ender
41. Make like Icarus
42. Puts on the staff
43. Cinderella's or Rocky's story, e.g.
47. Recover
48. Sarcastic laughs
52. Like some booms
54. Render unplayable, as a board
56. VIP at VMI
57. Ike or Abe, once
58. 1827 to 1 hand, hinted at by the starts of 17-, 26-, and 43-across
60. Gospel singer Winans
61. UAE part
62. Remove stitches from
63. Inquires about aces using Gerber, e.g.
64. Paris hub
65. Colorful aquarium fish

DOWN

1. Hearts, e.g.
2. Horseshoe-shaped lab item
3. Type of sax played by Bill Clinton
4. Acknowledge applause
5. Part of PST
6. Miffed
7. Gordie of hockey fame
8. "Hansel and Gretel" hot spot
9. Three, four, or five, usually
10. "Whenever"
11. Out of it
12. "Santa Baby" singer, 1953
13. SEA stats
18. Opponent of George and Bill
22. One of TV's "Golden Girls"
24. Elemental ending
25. Cannabis product
27. Cheri in "Scary Movie"
28. Negating link
29. Bridge world champion Lawrence
30. Often the best card to pull out
31. Radio-active one?
32. "M*A*S*H" star
33. Hooligan

Without Honor

37. Saw, say
38. Card game for two
39. Provider of a lucky break?
41. Legato's opp., in music
42. Sailor's pronoun
44. Grabs control of
45. Rubenesque
46. Xbox hit game
49. Not to be missed
50. "Gotcha"
51. One of two in Canada?
52. Org. concerned with lab safety
53. Metal-bearing minerals
54. "M*A*S*H" co-star

55. Ph.D. exam, often
58. 7'6" Ming
59. Same old same old

Across

1. Big mo. in Punxsutawney
4. Light weight
8. Pueblo people
13. "Like that'll ever happen!"
15. Org. defending Scopes
16. ___-garde
17. Suburban shopper's convenience
19. Martial artist who starred in "The One"
20. Goldfinger's sidekick
21. Cash cache (abbr.)
23. Iran's monetary unit
24. It comes out of a 21-across
25. One with an aversion to early retirement
27. Frank's second ex
29. Snookered, slangily
31. Confession starter
32. Great advancement for plantations
36. Goes from the one to the three level, e.g.
40. Smith or trump follower
41. Lollobrigida and Gershon
43. Lake not far from Niagara Falls
44. "___ can" (Obama campaign slogan)
46. College team's anthem
48. Mathematics degree?
50. ___ Paulo, Brazil
51. PBS funding source
52. Ring adornment
57. Math class, for short
59. Getting warm, say
60. PPO alternative
61. Coin-edge ridges
64. The movie "Wordplay", for example
66. Gruff creature?
68. "We" and "They", e.g.
69. Ancient Irish tongue
70. "Happy Motoring" sloganeer
71. One of the majors?
72. "___ ex machina"
73. Big name in fuel additives

Down

1. Burkina ___
2. Cornerstone abbr.
3. They might attract lorikeets
4. Like many a 3NT opener
5. "The most trusted name in electronics" sloganeer
6. Bridge champion Falk
7. 2D opener showing many different types of hands
8. Fifth pillar of Islam
9. Wins partner's king, e.g.
10. Place for a steak-out?
11. Acquired relation
12. Moonshine machine
14. Archipelago discovered by Tasman in 1643
18. Mexican menu choice
22. Studio with a roaring lion
26. Cock and bull?
27. ___-deucey
28. Sotto ___ (in a soft tone)
30. End-of-the-week letters

Small Slam in Clubs

33. He might ring a bell
34. Magician's name suffix
35. Hounds
37. Gymnastics pose requiring great strength
38. Have a nostalgic feeling for
39. Genesis creator?
42. Manacles
45. Afr. nation bordering Kenya
47. Go ___ length
49. "Like that'll ever happen!"
52. Purchase at a Jewish deli
53. First word of a counting rhyme

54. When said three times, et cetera
55. Set securely
56. Black, in Bordeaux
58. Sport in which competitors lie on their backs
62. Lowest in rank
63. Card with an exclamation point
65. It's not an exact fig.
67. Fighting Tigers of the NCAA

Across

1. Org. protecting air and water
4. Regarding
8. With 71-across, one of four in this puzzle
14. Guy's main squeeze
15. Practice with a palooka, perhaps
16. Send back pard's suit
17. Gets tiresome
19. 8-across saws, e.g.
20. Florida tribesman
21. RSVP piece
22. Office in the White House
23. End of the world?
27. They're not in the in crowd
29. Part of WWW
30. Bird's alma mater
32. Its symbol is a panda (abbr.)
34. Holds the minority opinion
38. Set one's sights
42. "King Kong" and "King Kong", e.g.
43. Faux fat used in some chips
44. Nightstand companion
45. Person who watches the kids?
47. Wonderboy, in "The Natural"
48. Heliocentric center
49. Whisper sweet nothings
51. Bowlful in many a dorm room
55. Dixie
60. Highball mixer
61. Org. funding many PBS programs
62. Reservations
64. Hit list?
67. Like some hounds
68. Veer
69. Tiger's ex
70. "... a man ___ mouse?"
71. See 8-across
72. Fender bender
73. Letters for a lawyer

Down

1. Needles
2. Containing no meat or milk, in Judaism
3. Sandy or Roberto of baseball
4. AARP or NAACP, e.g.
5. Service member?
6. Candle or soap base
7. Decreed
8. Full of chutzpah
9. Commit a faux pas with a chip
10. Author Calvino
11. Understood, slangily
12. Cousin of the SAT
13. Nav. officer
18. Scene for many an oater
24. Car the Beach Boys sang about
25. Golfer's turf
26. Lipstick lady Lauder
28. Lawnmower's track
31. Cold War initials
33. Prometheus stole it from Olympus
35. Many a Bosnian
36. Lipstick mishap
37. Hong Kong is part of it
38. Getup

Table for Four

39. Outspoken?
40. Cartoonist who created Billy, Dolly, Jeffy and P.J.
41. Polo, for one
46. Slapped down a red card, e.g.
50. "Lawrence of Arabia" star
52. Blonde whom gentlemen preferred
53. Landscaper's tools
54. NYSE rival
56. It helps with communication
57. Source of irritation

58. More rational
59. Cabbie's line
63. Smallville surname
64. Medicinal amt.
65. Pal of Pooh and Piglet
66. Shell-game element

ACROSS

1. Author Roald of "Matilda" and "The BFG"
5. Pointer's word
10. HQs
14. Fully fit to serve
15. Sports
16. Jalopy
17. Play a sure winner in second seat, e.g.
20. Big red for bridge, e.g.
21. Logically arranged, as the cards in one's hand
22. Female pronoun
23. Oft-mispunctuated pronoun
24. Make a splinter bid, e.g.
31. Muppet with a unibrow
32. Financier/philanthropist of fame
33. Garish, as some garments
35. Really dug
37. Barracks VIP
38. Man of Marseilles
39. Respond 3NT after pard opens 1C, e.g.
42. Uncouth sort
43. Online exchanges often including LOL and BRB
44. Mind a minor
45. Annual ACBL spring event
46. Palindromic celeb
47. E-mail subject line abbr.
49. Olympic category which the starts of 17-, 24-, and 39-across hint at
56. Bergen _____ (fit-showing convention)
57. Initials of obligation
58. Pedometer button
60. Bubbling
61. Mo. in which many a 52-down is sung
62. Take off the board
63. Screwy
64. Member of a fraternal order
65. Take effect

DOWN

1. Qatar's capital
2. Oft-quoted auth.?
3. Air filter acronym
4. "Har har, chuckles!"
5. Stymies an endplay, e.g.
6. "The Lost Boys" star Corey
7. Guinness Book suffix
8. Area in London or NYC
9. Means of transportation?
10. Edible holiday cylinder
11. Sprint
12. Many a 3NT contract, essentially
13. Sprinted
18. SAT practice
19. Cutting-edge component, briefly
24. Establish, as in a trick in a long suit
25. Krispy ___
26. Hollywood's B. D. and Anna May

27. Grp. with brass
28. Pillages villages
29. Salesman for the fictional Wagner Company
30. Diploma word, sometimes
31. Cabo's peninsula
34. ____ Finesse (contract evaluator)
36. Lavish
38. Starts, as in a grand theft auto
40. Assurance after a fall
41. Bit of a dustup
46. Haven
48. Farm implement pioneer

49. "The forbidden fragrance," in ads
50. Sidesplitter
51. White House worker
52. Song heard in 61-across
53. Smoothly play low
54. Test for many a college sr.
55. Big name in 50's comedy
56. Bid 6NT after opps doubled 6S, e.g.
59. Source of a hand upgrade, sometimes

Across

1. Grape used for burgundies
6. Wind or wit descriptor
12. Part of a drum kit, informally
17. Grab ___
18. Vaquero's place
19. Flavor similar to fennel
20. Masterpiece damaged in 1991 by a deranged man with a hammer
23. Taken for
24. Some riding mowers
25. Famous misquote from a classic film
30. Make unplayable, as a bridge board
32. Zigged and zagged
33. Coated with gold leaf
36. Sax section
38. Hard, in Havana
39. Not allow Time to run out?
40. Snag
41. Musical based on "The Taming of the Shrew"
46. End of a Fred Flintstone cry
47. Ethereal
48. Christian of fame?
50. Not beat around the bush, and a hint to the ends of 20-, 25-, and 41-across
58. Martial arts star of "Romeo Must Die"
59. Good defender's asset
60. Harden (to)
62. "Half ___ is better than none"
63. Main course
64. Film that really takes off?
65. Fleeting flash
66. Gentlemen (abbr.)
67. Little bit

Down

1. TV's Dawber
2. Sacred bird of the Pharaohs
3. "You read that green perfectly!"
4. Murderous Moor
5. "Lovergirl" singer Marie
6. São Paulo's land, to its natives
7. Creator of a famous James
8. Capt. Picard's series, to fans
9. Luge surface
10. Org. that plays its games on 9-down
11. Treat
12. Brother of Zeus and Poseidon
13. Going ballistic
14. Group think, a la The Borg
15. Purchase proviso
16. Shelley and Kirstie's "Cheers" co-star
21. Spreads (out), like dummy's hand
22. Telegraph, say
26. Little bits
27. One with a school tie
28. "An Inconvenient Truth" star
29. Frenzied way to run
30. Shoot the breeze?
31. Flamenco cheer
34. Zodiac creature
35. Low spot?

Who's the Boss?

37. One way to get to the top
39. Doubles after two passes, at times
42. Nest egg letters
43. Precision, for example
44. Bridge platitudes, e.g.
45. Third word in "America"
47. Falk who wrote "Spingold Challenge" and "Team Trial"
49. Increased excessively, as the score
50. Phone zone
51. Parisian possessive
52. Certain conifer

53. Figs.
54. ACBL event VIPs
55. Cabinet dept. created in 1977
56. Surfer's sobriquet
57. Jeff's partner for decades
58. Bender
61. Shriek from the funny pages

Across

1. Hideous ____ (Victor Mollo character)
4. NAP winner, e.g.
9. Like a useful suit in dummy, often
14. Gentle sort
18. Partnership agreement?
19. HCP source
20. Nuptial garb
21. "Eight ____..."
22. Ephemeral celebrity
26. "The Love Boat" mixologist
27. "____ expert, but ..."
28. Card game exclamation
29. Flummoxed
30. The one in a hole-in-one
32. RN workplaces
34. Fond du ____, WI
36. "For shame!" sound
37. 1984 film with Long Duk Dong
42. Catchall abbreviation
45. Ultimate degree
46. It's underfoot
47. It keeps one grounded
51. Teaser
53. "Xanadu" grp.
56. Some HDTVs and DVD players
58. "Ciao!"
59. Insects with a relatively long life cycle
63. It's between two and one for many bridge pairs
64. Create, as a statute
65. Mole, of sorts
66. Peruvian pronoun
67. Bog
68. Kicked in
69. Phoenix-rising sites
70. Babe's hangout?

Down

1. Audiophiles' buys
2. Keats, notably
3. Have lots of success
4. Monitor
5. Break ground?
6. Years, in Latin
7. Dearest woman
8. King's kin
9. "The Simpsons" character Disco ____
10. Certain Rwandan
11. Yoke mates
12. Like many a used car
13. General on a menu
14. LHO part
15. Nautical yell
16. Internet phenoms
17. 2-1 is usually a good one
23. New Mexico resort town
24. Heart and soul, e.g.
25. "Come on, get real!"
31. Abbr. on a business card

Point Spread

33. It's sometimes measured in IMPs
35. HS math subject
38. Famous last words?
39. "Li'l Abner" cartoonist
40. Almost
41. Whiskey spritz
42. Soaking salts
43. Famous fountain of film
44. Split one's honors, at times
48. Carnival sights
49. Breeze along
50. Exam composition
52. Scant

54. Ace from ace-king, e.g.
55. First word of many fairy tales
57. Fight souvenir?
60. Leaves in hot water?
61. Abbr. on a financial statement or a pay stub
62. Dvorak's "Symphony No. 9 ___ Minor"

ACROSS

1. Like a junkyard dog
5. Parapsychology term
8. SAT analogy words
12. Roomy places?
13. "The Big Easy" of golf
14. It's sometimes put down before jumping
15. Switch suits with the intent of stopping ruffs
18. "___ Boot"
19. Where Sherif Ali ibn el Kharish adventured
20. Sign up at an NABC, e.g.
24. WWF concern
25. Humbert Humbert's obsession
27. Some responses to Stayman, essentially
31. Pic to click
32. "Moving on then..."
35. On target
36. 4C and 4D after 1S-3S, perhaps
39. Word usually put in brackets
40. This point forward
41. Dunker's delight
43. Work boot features
47. Hawks at an NBA game?
50. Extremely fussy, slangily
51. Fail by a trick
55. Simmer slowly, as beef
56. West with zest
57. Take a finesse, e.g.
61. Californian vineyard valley
62. Somme time
63. Nautically sheltered
64. Bridge, essentially
65. "___ guy walks into a bar..."
66. Man with 5,714 K's

DOWN

1. Transgression
2. Augment
3. "Horrible Bosses" star
4. Fed. grant maker
5. Hamman who won a gold medal at the World Team Olympiad
6. NY hospital, ___-Kettering
7. Sanford of "The Jeffersons"
8. Barak, for one
9. Alphabet chunk that's a name
10. Jerry's tormentor
11. The O of LHO
16. Pave the way?
17. DVR alternative
21. Boy in 2000 headlines
22. Kind of battery, briefly
23. Sporty car features
26. One with a small nest egg?
28. Literary collection (abbr.)
29. Minstrel's strings
30. Like some club suits in a 1C opener
33. Faux butter
34. The O of old radio lingo
36. "Odyssey" temptress
37. Immense expanse
38. Antediluvian Peruvian
39. Redouble, sometimes
42. Brit's buddy
44. It's not the norm
45. Wonder drug

46. Make lustrous
48. Be catty?
49. Sudden outpourings
52. "Likewise!"
53. "Barbarella" actor Milo
54. Microscopic
57. The powers that be
58. Annual ACBL event for
    partners
59. Spring for a vacation?
60. Place for Peter Pan?

Across

1. Mom-and-pop orgs.?
5. Grill seasonings
9. Seasoning amt.
13. Ethiopian princess of opera
14. Capital of Yemen
15. Spread for bread
16. George's sitar teacher
17. It's a rap
19. Concede (to)
21. New Zealand parrot
22. Largest airport in OH
23. Wine lauded in "Sideways"
26. Dogpatch surname
28. TV's Lake
29. Dude (up)
31. Mulligan
32. Teutonic pronoun
33. "Family Feud" host of old
36. Starter home?
37. Head-on competition
39. Low-maintenance "pet"
42. Play catch, e.g.
43. Game with 52 cards
46. Jingled
47. First name in despotism
48. Stump
50. Nunavut native
52. Like an arrogant brat
55. Seattle summer hrs.
56. Cry from a crib
58. The Hustle's genre
59. Young bridge wunderkind, e.g.
62. Crochet, e.g.
65. Tales of old
66. Dig, so to speak
67. Nebraskan natives
68. Hollywood giants?
69. Red states, once (abbr.)
70. Table talk, e.g., and what's found in 17-, 23-, 37-, 52-, and 59-across

Down

1. ___ score (bridge term originating in golf)
2. Father's hermana
3. Raise pard's overcall, e.g.
4. Gave the nod
5. Left for, after being doubled, perhaps
6. Game with 108 cards
7. Places for many a deal
8. Japanese sauce?
9. Single, double, and triple follower
10. Sad suit state
11. Screen
12. Franchise whose characters have decorated an All Nippon Airways jet
14. Metaphorical stake
18. Norman who was Edgar Kaplan's longtime bridge partner
20. Sacred peak in Greek myth (abbr.)
23. Seven's trio, sometimes
24. Sequel's sequel?
25. "That's just wrong"
27. Cookie used in some stacking contests

Second Negative

30. Annoyance during a night game, perhaps
34. Not behind
35. Places where punishment is doled out
37. Biblical trio
38. Midnights' counterparts
39. Hamstring
40. One who's not often dummy, e.g.
41. Soon to be delivered, perhaps
43. Saw through
44. Put away the dishes?
45. Vulnerable

49. "You go, girl!"
51. Number of keycards 5S indicates, usually
53. Sure targets?
54. Sticking point?
57. Latin trio member
60. "Super Mario Bros." console
61. Logic gate type
63. It can have its pluses
64. Name on many Chinese menus

Across

1. Kitty
4. Contract that might attract a Lightner double
8. Eat, slangily
14. Noise heard after uncovering a 6-0 split, perhaps
15. Actress Kunis of "That '70s Show"
16. "It's a Wonderful Life" family man
17. Having a face only a mother could love
19. High-priority, like a trump return to stop impending ruffs
20. _____-forcing 1NT
21. Reagan Secretary of State Alexander
23. U.S. govt. bond
24. Rorschach image
26. Those, in Tijuana
28. Run, as a side suit
30. It often gets stuck
35. "You've Got Mail" co.
36. ___ Islands (Nassau setting)
38. Run, as from NT to a suit contract
39. Naturalist on California quarters
41. Sic on
42. Homonym of 38-across
43. Star of 2009's "Star Trek"
44. Cara and Castle
46. Haute couture initials
47. Makeup of some watertight garments
49. Operates with a beam
51. Ira Corn's hired guns
52. Ark-itect?
53. Lustful being of myth
56. Scorsese flick of 2011
59. Mortgage adjustment, for short
62. Explored for 4-across, perhaps
64. Declarer's NT assets, and something this puzzle has three of (at the starts of 17-, 30-, and 47-across)
66. Like some Google Maps views
67. Hamilton alternative (abbr.)
68. Opus ___ ("The Da Vinci Code" group)
69. They come from Mars
70. On a slow boat to China, perhaps
71. Puzzle finisher's cry

Down

1. Litter contents
2. Give a long once-over
3. Teeny-weeny fairy-tale girl
4. Big D school
5. First-seat 1S opener holding Axxxx Kxx Qxx Jx, e.g.
6. ___ breve
7. Permission solicitation
8. ___ Simbel (Egyptian site)
9. It grows with every shot
10. Stops in a partial
11. It might be on a roll
12. Musical based on "La Bohème"
13. 8 bits, commonly
18. Monster of the Mojave?
22. People reunified in 1990
25. Symbol of royal power

There's a Hole in the Bucket

27. Be a slacker, slangily
28. Some summer youth bridge programs
29. Unlucky one in Frank Stewart's fictional club
30. Hold dear, as a good partner
31. Grainy?
32. "WarGames" and "Short Circuit" actress
33. Prolific bridge author of "What Would You Bid?"
34. Hands out hands
37. Just about identical
40. Component of Lebensohl, e.g.
45. ___-mo replay
48. Thigh-slapper

50. Org. with online bridge on its website
52. Nary a soul
53. Inbox clogger
54. Integration calculation
55. In a quandary, as whether to bid 4-across or not
57. Food stamp org.?
58. Classic muscle cars
60. ____ finesse (forced return after some endplays)
61. Fertility goddess of the Nile
63. Rosters of injured athletes, for short
65. School booster grp.

Across

1. Green of the Austin Powers films
5. Sired, biblically
10. Deer sir?
14. High-performance Camaro model
15. Home of bridge enthusiast Warren Buffett
16. "Peanuts" fussbudget
17. "Chill out!"
20. Greet the villain, say
21. 50 for the ____ (after making a doubled contract)
22. Birth name indicator
24. Seventh in a Greek series
25. "Everyone has to chip in"
34. East-west and north-south, e.g.
35. Number of cards held in a suit, for some preference bids
36. Sharply hit baseball
37. ___ mater
38. Quiet corners
40. Poet St. Vincent Millay
41. They often provide the most joy in life
44. Declare
45. "That hurts!" blurts
46. It has quite a twist (abbr.)
47. Legal attachment?
48. Signs off, for short
49. Head-slapping utterance
51. Letterman segment which might show a dog pushing another dog in a toy car
60. Hidden mike
61. Lotus-___ ("Odyssey" figure)
62. Ben Cohen or Terence Reese, e.g.
63. Similar (to)
64. Hindu maxim
65. High diamond?
66. Acronym for the starts of 17-, 25-, 41-, and 51-across
67. Professor in "The Nutty Professor"
68. ACBL system for some adherents of 66-across

Down

1. Certain Punjabi
2. Part of a Napoleonic palindrome
3. The "ten" in "hang ten"
4. Deal's 40 (abbr.)
5. Soft shoe?
6. Feature of Australia's coat of arms
7. Needle-toothed fish
8. Sighed sounds
9. Gauguin's getaway
10. Some shooters, for short
11. Something a person may take a spin in?
12. System written about by Cohen and Reese
13. Grieg's "Peer ___"
18. Pulls, as from 3NT doubled
19. Collectively
23. Legally impedes
24. Produced a vivid impression of

Back to the Basics

25. "No bid"
26. Sylvester's "Rocky" costar
27. Lassie's TV owner
28. Get ___ on the knuckles
29. MP's pursuit
30. Substitution word
31. First name of Fezzik's portrayer in "The Princess Bride"
32. Hand-me-downs, of a sort
33. Wipe out, as a lead
38. Anchor's place
39. It's sometimes blasted out of
42. Valhalla villain
43. Reptilian suffix

48. Employs Gambling 3NT, e.g.
50. Rubes
51. Love letters?
52. Backyard party torch
53. Author of "Exodus"
54. Soloway who won five Bermuda Bowls
55. Dramatic rebuke
56. Stretch in a seat
57. ___ Obama (product marketed in 2009)
58. Singer Perry with the 2010 #1 hit "California Gurls"
59. Guideline, briefly

SECTION 2:
MEDIUM

**

ACROSS

1. Ristorante's "in the style of"
5. Not just sniffle
9. Key of Brahms's Piano Trio No. 1
13. Legendary late-night host
14. Spread out on a table?
15. It's a piece of cake
16. Pass with points after RHO's opener, perhaps
17. Gung-ho quality
18. Safekeeping site
19. Rock group?
20. AKQJ AKQJ AK KJ9, e.g.
22. Passenger of the 60-down
24. It comes straight from the heart
25. AKQJ AKQJ AK KJ9, e.g.
29. MiB extras
32. Had a list
33. Whiffenpoof, e.g.
35. Shade by the beach?
38. AKQJ AKQJ AK KJ9, e.g.
41. Hurdle for an aspiring JD
42. LeVar's "Roots" role
44. Part of many a bridge movement
46. Fish-sticks fish
47. AKQJ AKQJ AK KJ9, e.g.
53. The gold, in Guadalajara
55. "Holy cow!"
56. Man dealt AKQJ AKQJ AK KJ9 by James Bond
61. Some PCs
62. Admiral _____ of "Star Wars"
63. Saturnine
64. Slimming option, for short
65. Houdini's birth name
66. Suit quality that often calls for an upgrade
67. "Why should ___ you?"
68. Squat
69. Descartes quote word
70. Number of tricks 56-across took when defending 7C redoubled

DOWN

1. Quality of many a top bridge player
2. Olympic wreath
3. Border city on the Rio Grande
4. Place for lucky pairs
5. Chucklehead
6. He plays Jack on "30 Rock"
7. Like some jump-shifts
8. "I Can Haz Cheezburger?" critter
9. Jump to slam without using RKCB, e.g.
10. It has a Mini-Maxi variant
11. Sore spot
12. Raspberry, e.g.
15. Scamper
20. Croupier's instrument
21. Potential perch
23. Showy display of brilliance
26. Scoring format in some NABC events
27. Game with red cards
28. Obeys a red card

30. "Wayne's World" actress Carrere
31. Defeat, as a partial
34. However, familiarly
35. Pedigree-tracking org.
36. ___ vadis
37. Miss a cold game, e.g.
39. Take a place at a table
40. The day before the big day
43. Dangerous liaisons, often
45. Serengeti antelope
48. ACBL follower on the internet?
49. Noggin
50. Quite some time
51. Dog in the RCA Victor logo
52. Pizarro contemporary
54. Capital city whose name means "place of the gods"
56. Cut, in a way
57. Chain founded by Ingvar Kamprad
58. Swinger at a saloon
59. It helps you get a leg up
60. Carrier of 22-across
64. Jack's "30 Rock" underling

Across

1. Bidding followers?
6. Smelly
10. Like some tables at finals
14. First name in philanthropy
15. Greek lover boy?
16. The Big Easy, briefly
17. Jordan, Cooper, and Finley?
20. Game ___
21. Tempeh eater, perhaps
22. Lash ___ (berate)
23. Badlands formation
24. Mouth-puckering
26. Bungee-jumping teens?
32. Whizzes
33. Sites for studs
34. Have a date, say
36. Name of four Holy Roman emperors
37. Light brown tint
39. Ex-Yankee Martinez
40. It may be loaded
41. DDE's alma mater
42. City whose name means "eastern capital"
43. Upward move after "You're hired!", perhaps?
47. Do high-tech surgery on
48. De ___ of films
49. Old Testament verse
52. Brosnan's co-star in "The Thomas Crown Affair"
54. Price to pay
57. Coup d'etat?
60. "Voilà!"
61. Grew older (and wiser)
62. Pick on
63. "Ain't that the truth!"
64. First name of a Parisian stinker
65. Made a choice

Down

1. Make tracks
2. 0 letters
3. It might reveal a bad break
4. "The Purloined Letter" monogram
5. Trembles
6. Ska relative
7. "Joy of Cooking" writer Rombauer
8. Leader, of a sort
9. Upper-left key, often
10. Acting without thinking
11. Job involving much stress
12. First name in scat
13. 19th-century Harper's Weekly cartoonist
18. Oriole's home
19. They're locked in battle
23. Post-it note, e.g.
25. Ethereal
26. Polo rival
27. Tag cry
28. Caster, of a sort
29. Name on many a Scotch bottle
30. Japanese therapeutic touch technique
31. Japanese electronics giant
35. SpongeBob, e.g.

37. Dosage abbr.
38. Current measurement
39. Famous film terrier
41. Proposed "fifth taste"
42. Master Point Press setting
44. Tracey on whose show "The Simpsons" debuted
45. It's kind of a kick
46. Paste in Asian cookery
49. Org. that supports fake fur
50. Endpoint of many an exploration
51. Radar O'Reilly, e.g.

53. Sch. near the Rio Grande
54. 4-3-3-3, e.g.
55. Mitigate
56. Sized up
58. Annual ACBL event
59. Liveliness

Across

1. Facebook measure of support
5. 28-down bidder, sometimes
11. Ancient symbol of life
15. Spelling of "Beverly Hills 90210"
16. Flotilla
17. ___ cava
18. World leader who played bridge
21. Bird in "Peter and the Wolf"
22. Good thing for declarer to have
23. Snow White and the Seven Dwarfs, e.g.
24. FDR New Deal agency
26. Piece activists? (abbr.)
27. World leader who played bridge
35. Hoodwinks
36. Cloaked
37. Reliever's goal
39. Teddy's Mt. Rushmore neighbor
40. Many a self-professed expert's problem
42. Billy goat's bleat
43. World leader who played bridge
46. Animal that sleeps upside-down
47. Seemingly forever
48. Brouhahas
49. Contents of la mer
51. One of the fam
52. World leader who played bridge
58. Deschapelles, e.g.
60. Gave temporarily
61. Dinghy thingies
64. 51-across of Cain
65. As a whole
66. VIP at a 63-down
67. Play second hand high, e.g.
68. Shade of pink
69. "Family Guy" creator MacFarlane

Down

1. Former Fords
2. "Music Man" setting
3. Singer whose first name starts his last name
4. Pizza slices, often
5. Morsel for Mr. Ed
6. Get set, briefly
7. Oscar-winning Jannings
8. "Discovery" grp.
9. Site of an early cover-up?
10. Bid over a double, perhaps
11. Shade of green
12. Lizardlike creature
13. Bender, of a sort
14. Stag
19. Jewish folk song, "___ Nagila"
20. Game ender, perhaps
25. Words after touch or stop
26. Bottom
27. Oil company in a 1999 merger
28. Balanced bridge bid, briefly
29. Go on and on and on

Top Players

30. Transmission repair chain
31. Hall of Fame southpaw Warren
32. Taxonomic term
33. Like a rainforest
34. Author Calvino
35. Calls in a field
38. "Do the Right Thing" pizzeria
40. Green Mountain Boys' Allen
41. When Romeo and Juliet have their balcony scene
44. Index fingers, in a kids' rhyme
45. Works the room
50. Not-so-cute fruit
51. Gazpacho eater's need
52. ACBL annual fees
53. "Warrior Princess" of TV
54. IMF part
55. Subject of a real Bohr?
56. Name of four Holy Roman emporers
57. 5D, e.g.
58. One for the road?
59. "Memoirs of a Geisha" wardrobe item
62. Go bad
63. See 66-across

Across

1. Trump
5. Made like Pan
10. Bazillions
14. "La Bamba" star Morales
15. Dean Martin song topic
16. Dogie catcher
17. American car only made from 1994-1997, which cars.com reviewed as "merely adequate"
19. What high-low might signal
20. Last word in many ultimatums
21. Interminably
22. Bridge teacher Harrington
25. It's often used to damn things up
29. They're unstressed
31. "Iliad" god who favored the Trojans
32. Estar partner
33. Cry of epiphany
34. Boss suit, so to speak
35. ___-relief
36. Unescapable end
40. Internists' org.
42. Pequod's crew
43. Joint Web project
46. ___ es Salaam
47. Snerd's seat
48. Drag
50. Common ultimate frisbee injury
53. It changes locks
54. Prepared to be shot
55. Take the prescribed number of tricks
57. It's out on a limb
58. Bridge event type, and a hint to the circled letters
64. Cry of accomplishment
65. Like Bo Peep's flock
66. Tiff
67. 1988 Cy Young winner Hershiser
68. Basic religious belief
69. He loved Maria in "West Side Story"

Down

1. He might cry foul (abbr.)
2. It offered Hope
3. Way off
4. Bona ___
5. Assume the identity of
6. Pyramid architect of fame (abbr.)
7. Island staple
8. Overbid, e.g.
9. "Gidget" star Sandra
10. NBA venue
11. Age-old adage
12. It's far out
13. Formally offers
18. "A" in radio lingo
21. 1987 World Champion skater Brian
22. Letter resembling a trident
23. Some GE appliances
24. Luke's temptation
26. Onetime foe of the recording industry
27. Lobsterman's gear
28. Mani's partner

His & Hers

30. Teeny-tiny
34. Lug
37. Popped the question
38. Gets some color
39. "Isn't that the cutest thing?"
40. Go with the flow
41. Venomous ocean dweller
44. Cryptographer's aid
45. Acrimony
48. Royal headwear
49. Doing kitchen duty, to a G.I.
51. Kosher
52. Church approvals
56. Defender, about half the time

58. Like a fashionista
59. "___been had!"
60. It's atop many faces
61. Google had one in Aug. 2004
62. Played all ones trumps, e.g.
63. Sloppy digs

Across

1. Small dams
6. Breakers of zero tolerance, perhaps
11. Call letters?
14. Llama's kin
15. Actress Davis of the "Matrix" movies
16. John L. Lewis org.
17. Compressors, of a sort
19. Toll rd.
20. Respond 2H to pard's 1H, e.g.
21. Sacrifice, e.g.
22. 1980s rap trio Run-___
25. It's all charged up
29. "Headlines" presenter
31. Sweats with head coverings
32. ___ spell (relax)
33. Begin, as bad weather
34. Full days at the ballpark, and what the first parts of 17-, 25-, 49-, and 56-across are
40. Joyously
41. Bridge position
43. Colonial home?
46. Like good defense against NT slams, usually
49. Brandi Chastain's 1999 shot of fame
51. Old name preceder
52. Novel idea?
53. Chinese leader Zhou ___
55. 58-down by the space bar
56. Chinese, often
62. What a psyche is, in a way
63. Caught a few z's
64. Finish using TurboTax, say
65. Nessman of "WKRP in Cincinnati"
66. It's beyond deep
67. Name associated with classic rock, or poetry

Down

1. London lavs (abbr.)
2. ___ de cologne
3. Unit for many an NABC event
4. Not an orig.
5. Everett of "Citizen Kane"
6. "Bid already, pard!"
7. "Ulysses" actor Milo
8. Troop grp.
9. 1999 Frank McCourt memoir
10. "Get my drift?"
11. When Caesar asks "Et tu, Brute?"
12. Be sneaky?
13. Commuter's buy
18. It means nothing in Nantes
21. Rubicundity
22. Some WKRP characters
23. Picker-upper?
24. Prefix meaning "cell"
26. You, biblically
27. Extremely small amount
28. A splinter might show it
30. Jeer
33. A little short
35. Respond to an SOS redouble, with "out"
36. Spirited air
37. Jed Clampett's daughter

Twice as Nice

38. Hold your horses?
39. Bid 7C over opps' 6NT, e.g.
42. Kickoff platform
43. Shock
44. Nervous ___
45. Some govt. securities
46. Some reds
47. Org. that fights censorship
48. Went around in circles, perhaps
50. Holds onto during a squeeze, as Jxxx
54. Like some 24-point 3NT games
56. JFK examiners
57. Liturgical vestment
58. 55-across, e.g.
59. Pipeline product
60. Pay attachment?
61. Man cave, perhaps

Across

1. Suit involved in a Drury exploration
6. Home repair guru Bob
10. Scottish hillside
14. A bit of lowlife?
15. Related (to)
16. "Quack" component
17. "I made that tricky contract!"
18. First name in jeans
19. Tribe related to the Iowa
20. Tax form fig.
21. Kwik-E-Mart clerk
23. Life Master level after diamond
25. Like many a 24 point 3NT contract
27. Perambulate
28. Queen 57-across in a Disney movie
29. Pickler's herb
30. Support, of a sort
33. J. Edgar Hoover employees
35. Abbr. at the top of sheet music
36. Possible outcome of a RKCB exploration
37. Olympic speeder
38. Marisa of "The Wrestler"
40. User-edited site
41. Frankfurter's cries
42. One with a habit
43. Earned, as IMPs
45. RR depot purchase
46. What many beginners must muster up to double for business
47. Mate of a 34-down
48. Humorist Sahl
49. Like many bridge pairs who go against the field
52. "Unfortunately, we went down..."
55. King ___ (5NT, often)
56. London lav
57. 28-across, e.g.
58. Channel for armchair QBs
60. Merger acquisition?
62. "Money ___ object"
63. Interpret, or interpreted
64. Nut case?
65. Jury member, theoretically
66. Goes off course
67. ___ a fox

Down

1. Palindromic title
2. Commodore computer introduced in 1985
3. See 4-down
4. ___-Wan Kenobi, 3-down
5. Capable of being appraised
6. Appraiser's determination
7. DDE's nickname
8. Dynamo
9. Concern concerning boxers' welfare
10. Reykjavik-born one-named singer
11. Pro ___
12. Bidding system common in Britain
13. Barely made (out), as a 4 HCP response

Switching Things Up

22. Place for perennial propagation
24. Expansion wing
26. Willie of "Charles in Charge"
29. Denounces
30. Unproductive undertaking
31. Despicable sort
32. Betwixt and between
33. Hand without a five-card suit, e.g.
34. Mate of a 47-across
36. Despicable sort
39. Cruising, as on a bridge cruise

44. Something thrown on many red carpets
46. Saturn, for one
48. Inverted subject in the puzzle's circled letters
49. Smooths out
50. Denizen of Down Under
51. Cat calls?
52. Cheeky
53. Go up with the ace, e.g.
54. Primo
59. Print maker?
61. Kings' grp.

Across

1. Humdrum
5. South's pal North, e.g.
9. Stylish
13. Hero of Hinduism
14. AARP member?
15. Peace Prize winner Walesa
16. Bridge champion Sontag
17. ___ de gallo
18. Jai ___
19. Ballast unit
21. Wrestler's worry
23. Quote by Lee Hazen, part 1
25. Crime scene evidence (abbr.)
26. Org. of concern to AARP
27. "The Godfather: Part II" setting
30. "Maybe, maybe not"
35. With 37-across, bridge player's dread
36. Quote, part 2
37. See 35-across
38. Pirate's place
40. Particulars
41. Anthem contraction
42. Powdery evidence
43. Quote, part 3
50. Group with a lot of hits
51. Card or double preceder
52. Disorderly stack
53. Bridge expert Helgemo
55. First name in linguistics
56. To be in a faraway land?
57. Brewer's kiln
58. Raced
59. 14-across counterpart in football
60. Utmost degrees
61. Discharge

Down

1. Luca who slept with the fishes
2. Show that had its Dey in court?
3. GE competitor
4. No question about it
5. Seedy tropical fruit
6. Compadre
7. Remote button abbr.
8. Is overwhelmed by
9. Declarer's assertion
10. Hägar the Horrible's wife
11. Carl famous for hostile takeovers
12. Casino IOU
20. Cause of misery
22. "By Jove!"
24. Leads to a seat
27. General found on some Chinese menus
28. European high spot
29. It's a groundbreaking tool
30. Hub once known as Orchard Field
31. Play for raised stakes
32. MLB division
33. "Forrest Gump" locale, slangily
34. Kvetchers' cries
36. It takes care of some undesirables
39. Fair to middling
40. Amazon.com fig.
42. Pulls out a blue card

Zzzzz...

43. Angle symbol
44. Red card, e.g.
45. Coerce
46. Gorilla-like
47. Doom's partner
48. Pong maker
49. '69 champ, briefly
50. Storyteller's link
54. "Dig in!"

Across

1. One of a queen's two (abbr.)
4. Make evident
10. Work meas.
14. Letters surrounded by a red oval
15. Dr. Seuss character with a red hat
16. Southernmost Great Lake
17. Needling defenders while preparing for an endplay?
19. Mystique
20. Cake finisher
21. NASA sci.
22. Govt. agent
23. Declarer maneuver which makes a defender miserable
26. Shred to pieces
28. Person obsessed with aces and voids?
32. Young '___ (little folk)
35. Dust Bowl migrant
36. Aromatic wood used for chests
37. Crunch at an IGA
39. Deer sirs?
42. iPhone attendant
43. Gave up a seat
45. Big bore
47. Super ___ (Nintendo system)
48. Bridge player who thrives on zeros?
52. Tree with chocolate-yielding seeds
53. Blue Angel, e.g.
57. ACBL event spread out across a large area
59. "Curses!"
61. Mexican earthenware vessel
62. First name in communism
63. "We whacked them for 800!" and such?
66. Pakistani tongue
67. Feelings of dissatisfaction
68. Pop in on
69. Section of St. Peter's
70. Do a second draft
71. Athletes Cobb and Detmer

Down

1. Possesses a "je ne sais quoi"
2. Great guy, to some
3. Kitchen utensil
4. Mysterious "gift" (abbr.)
5. Part of a still
6. "That was no joke, buddy!"
7. Long and Vardalos
8. He overthrew Batista in 1959
9. Chef known to "kick it up a notch"
10. Assets of a hand
11. Stopped declarer from cashing a side suit winner, e.g.
12. Italian bread, once
13. Head, slangily
18. High-performance Camaro model
24. Wine and dine, say
25. Signs on the dotted line
27. Certain GI
29. Aptly named English novelist
30. Bern's river

Bridge on the Mind 1

31. 1990's rap duo ___ Kross
32. School north of LA
33. Gp. created in 1949
34. They make up many echoes
38. "You got me"
40. Steal, in a way
41. "We" or "They", on scorepads
44. ER VIP
46. WPM part
49. More steamed up
50. E.g.
51. Dig like a pig
54. Jump directly to 6D, e.g.

55. Film noir setting
56. Accepts
57. Arctic seabird
58. It sometimes covers a diamond
60. Selma, to Maggie
64. Back talk
65. Taiwan or Japan suffix

ACROSS

1. "Sweet ___" (Sally's pet name for Linus)
6. Chinese for "water"
10. Providence art sch.
14. Throw for ___
15. British pound, informally
16. "Hairy man" of Genesis
17. Executive earnings, often
20. Jiff
21. ACBL subdivision
22. Boxer's protest
23. Garten of the Food Network
24. Lead convention from xxx (abbr.)
25. 15th century Hungarian cavalrymen
28. They can be drawn or drawn through
30. Like some generals and hotels
31. Where salts go
32. Y chromosome carrier
33. Test track section
34. Where one might need a wake-up call (like the one at the starts of 17-, 30-, 46-, and 56-across)
38. In the style of
41. Good fellers?
42. Motionless
46. "Please drop in!"
49. "Full House" star
50. Like a proud papa's chest
51. Get up and go
52. Oklahoma Native American
53. Reared
54. Spherical opening?
55. Amontillado holder
56. Still in it to win it
60. Popular pop
61. Ixnay
62. Sorta
63. He played Obi-Wan
64. Caved in
65. Short stories they're not

DOWN

1. Charles Mingus, e.g.
2. Completely unknown by
3. It comes up 1/36 of the time, on average
4. "Pow!" response
5. Britain-China conflict of old
6. It attacked the "Nautilus"
7. On the DL?
8. One-eighty, slangily
9. First name in tyranny
10. Reading nook, perhaps
11. Employ a scissors coup, essentially
12. Pete known for his outstanding service
13. Payable
18. African beasts with curved horns
19. The Big Board, briefly
25. Motocross obstacles
26. Bit of eye makeup?
27. BMOCs, often
29. EMT's device
30. ACBL Hall-of-_____
32. Reached the limit, with "out"
35. It hangs around

Wake-up Call

36. Splits hairs
37. Some nuclear material
38. Summer coolers, for short
39. Uncalled-for insult, say
40. 1927 Kafka novel
43. Chewing the scenery
44. Jefferson Memorial feature
45. 1992 Clinton rival
47. "Yo", in craps lingo
48. Adjective for a shoppe
49. Highway heavyweight
51. Souchong alternative
54. Rec room centerpiece (abbr.)

56. It may be worth 47-down, but not in bridge
57. Ballpark fig.
58. PBS benefactor
59. Seoul Soul maker

Across

1. Money made by a con
6. Copper, so to speak
10. Badlands Natl. Park site
14. Big wheels' wheels
15. Roughly
16. Valuable vein
17. Martinelli's product
19. Eastern pooh-bah
20. Partnership _____
21. Checkout lines? (abbr.)
22. Brown of "Good Eats"
23. Conned
25. "Aim High" sloganeer
28. Eastern pooh-bah
32. Desmond of "Sunset Boulevard"
33. It tops a queen
34. What an infrequent bridge player might show
36. Descartes' deduction
39. Almost no possibility
43. Former Sov. unit
44. Is hip to
45. Prefix meaning "vinegar"
46. Mushroom popular in Asian cuisine
49. Issue an embarrassing retraction
51. "Interview With the Vampire" author
54. CBS show with many spinoffs
55. Detox setting
56. School lobby org.
58. Humdrum
62. Big-mouthed pitcher
63. Nice feature to have, seen in 17-, 25-, 39-, and 51-across
66. Buzz's lunar partner
67. Word in some sch. names
68. Harmon of "Law & Order"
69. Pretentiously cultured
70. Become a stinker
71. Macho men

Down

1. Ziploc competitor
2. Stinking
3. Scoring syst. rewarding safety plays
4. Pecos Bill or Paul Bunyan
5. Monogram of Prufrock's creator
6. Belladonna or Galileo, e.g.
7. Jong who wrote "Fear of Flying"
8. Ollie North's onetime org.
9. Turning point of many ballets?
10. Weaving course?
11. One who whips a boxer into shape
12. Formed for a particular purpose
13. Bil of the funny pages
18. Hirsch of "Taxi"
22. Chad's loc.
24. Santa ____ (California winds)
26. Bidding 7NT after 1NT-3NT, e.g.
27. Campus service org.
28. BWI info
29. Smyrna fruits

It's a Feature!

30. Scale that's not absolute
31. Like many "Twilight Zone" episodes
35. Sky light? (abbr.)
37. X-___: tool brand
38. Persian greeting?
40. Polynesian amulet figure
41. Pillboxes, e.g.
42. Bidding that results in a 2-2 trump fit, e.g.
47. Just about
48. Royal ball
50. Berry touted as a superfood
51. Place to play

52. More advanced
53. Type in, as traveler results
57. Big game pursuer?
59. Newman's Own rival
60. Litmus test possibility
61. They may lead to hives
63. Vote (for)
64. OAS member
65. Law men (abbr.)

Across

1. Hand without HCPs
5. Santa's reindeer, e.g.
10. Where people get steamed?
13. Symbol of enduring life
14. What clubs in a 1C opener might be
15. Makeup kit item
16. Close calls
18. Mountain range between Europe and Asia
19. Egg holder
20. Woman's name meaning "lionlike"
21. Dictionary's upside-down "e"
24. Greek temple dedicated to Athena
27. World Cup standout Chastain
29. Sumatran swingers
30. Prefix meaning "gas"
31. Arizona sticker
34. Outing combining food and entertainment
39. Glass raiser's words
40. Garage sale stipulation
42. Hoppin' John ingredient
45. Start of a Beatles refrain
47. Ready to pop by, perhaps
50. 1930s refugees
51. A politician's primary concern?
52. Freak hand features, perhaps
54. Massive walker in "The Empire Strikes Back"
55. Common change of suit, and a clue to the circled letters
60. Bridge Bulletin fodder
61. Has a flat?
62. Bout of debauchery
63. Hard rock connectors?
64. Bacon product
65. It sometimes tells partner what not to lead

Down

1. Forbid, as smoking in the playing area
2. One abroad?
3. Offshoot of reggae music
4. Made the victim of an endplay
5. HAZMAT regulators
6. Nestling's call
7. Notorious skater Harding
8. UK opponent in the Falklands War
9. Rehab symptoms, for short
10. What a 1C opening hand might be
11. Roll players?
12. Part of the Panama palindrome
15. One worth two
17. TNT spot
20. Sacred city of Tibet
21. Entrepreneur-aiding org.
22. Rep on the street
23. Famous name in spydom
25. Author Philip and bridge champion Alvin
26. Faithfully following
28. Summer cooler

A Major Change

1	2	3	4		5	6	7	8	9			10	11	12
13					14						15			
16	◯	◯	◯	17	◯						18			
		19						20						
21	22	23				24	◯	25	26	◯	◯			
27					28			29						
30					31	32	33							
	34			35		◯	◯	◯	◯	◯		36	37	38
		39									40			41
	42	43	44					45	46					
47		◯	◯	◯	◯	◯	48	49		50				
51						52		53						
54				55	56	◯	◯	◯	◯			57	58	59
60				61						62			
63				64						65			

32. Cacophonous, as a crowd
33. El operator
35. Buns may cover them
36. Discuss bridge with fellow players after a session, e.g.
37. Morales of "NYPD Blue"
38. Let it ____ (take a finesse)
41. Maggie, to Bart and Lisa, familiarly
42. Large bills, informally
43. Senators' site
44. Improves one's edge?
46. Muscle mag displays
47. One no Trump?

48. Dale of oaters
49. Heart hookup
53. Diminutive, informally
55. Old Eur. realm
56. Many MIT grads
57. Bridge champion Rubin, nicknamed "The Beast"
58. OT enders, often
59. Cobb of baseball and Warner of toys

Across

1. Buffett ___
4. Victorian type
9. Motormouth's "gift"
12. Words before tear or lark
13. Intensifies
15. Pamplona plaudit
16. Nursery rhyme opener
19. Best Angler and Best Bowler, e.g.
20. First name in mausoleums
21. Starts with the top of a sequence, e.g.
22. Org. with an annual "Big Dance"
23. Mount climbed by Moses
25. Smell ___
26. Person who says "You darn kids have it easy these days", perhaps
29. First mate?
30. Decline, as at the end of a long session
31. Irritated to no end
35. Splintered, e.g.
40. "Seinfeld" stand-in phrase
46. Beginning of a conclusion
47. In plain sight
48. ABC plug
49. In the public eye
50. "___ intended"
51. Puncture sound
52. Contract symbolically within 16-, 26-, and 40- across
55. Gambler's lament
57. J and K, e.g.
58. Garlicky dressing
61. TV host Matt
62. Printemps follower
63. Passing a 100% forcing bid, e.g.
64. Much, slangily
65. "Spring ahead" letters
66. Elegance

Down

1. Larry who wrote "Bridge Below the Belt"
2. Maintainer of the World Heritage List (abbr.)
3. Online purchase facilitator
4. One hoofing it, for short
5. Fisherman's bane
6. Natural high?
7. Record holders?
8. Stop
9. French filmmaker Jean-Luc
10. Like some suckers
11. Suffix with harte- or wilde-
13. Trash-talk
14. S on an invitation
17. Bridge partners, e.g.
18. Like an unreachable winner in dummy
23. RAV4, e.g.
24. Lupino of "High Sierra"
27. Cheese cured in brine
28. Like a 5-0 split
31. Words from the pros
32. Shipping weight deduction
33. Beats by half a board, e.g.
34. Stunners, of a sort

	1	2	3			4	5	6	7	8			9	10	11
12					13						14		15		
16			17									18			
19						20				21					
22					23			24		25					
	26			27					28						
			29				30								
31	32	33	34						35	36	37	38	39		
40				41	42	43	44	45							
46				47						48					
49				50						51					
	52		53					54							
55	56				57			58			59	60			
61					62			63							
64					65			66							

36. Humbly takes the blame, as for a bidding accident
37. Alert
38. They often elicit both groans and stares (abbr.)
39. Insignificant amounts
41. In the distance, poetically
42. Steered clear of, as the danger hand
43. Goes off, as from normal conventions
44. Prop for Animal of "The Muppet Show"
45. Abbreviation in chemistry

53. Bonus, in adspeak
54. Glasgow negatives
55. Not up to par
56. Language of Indochina
59. Not quite ROFLMAO
60. Red state?

Across

1. Pull on, as heartstrings
6. Mixed-team tourney
11. Save against a slam, for short
14. Digital party planning aid
15. Half a Wonka character
16. ___-Magnon
17. Much of a brain's makeup
19. Home of the Buckeyes (abbr.)
20. Unfortunate
21. Nobel novelist Morrison
22. Privy to
23. The Gospels kick it off
27. Brewpubs
30. "Drat!"
31. Chews (on)
32. Toyota SUVs
36. Affirmative words
37. Covered with spots
39. Pet peeve?
40. Bombed, as a joke
42. Gone up in the rankings
43. Catchall abbr.
44. Life Master level between Diamond and Platinum
46. The Mongols, notably
50. In a frenzied fashion
51. "Major" attraction in the skies
52. Au ___
55. Jazz great Evans
56. Exercise equipment simulating skiing
60. NATO part
61. Tearjerker of a sort
62. Lunar lander of 1969
63. Culinary general?
64. Corporate shake-up, for short
65. Scarecrow's innards

Down

1. Honors worth no HCPs
2. Pigmented eye part
3. Reinforce
4. Off-road wheels, briefly
5. Isn't stable
6. Board's 40
7. Perez of "Do the Right Thing"
8. Mantra sounds
9. "The Simpsons" Kwik-E-Mart operator
10. West from Brooklyn
11. Tea biscuit
12. Heated crime?
13. Signal often given when following suit to declarer's lead
18. Word with ghost or boom
22. Utterance from a hot-handed player
23. Unauthorized release of information
24. Peeved
25. Hitting-the-ground sound
26. Raggedy doll
27. End of the week acronym
28. Kitty feeder
29. Rocky Mountains resort
32. Blackwood ask, and a hint to an appropriate number of answers in the puzzle
33. "Born Free" lioness
34. React to an uppercut, perhaps
35. Hourglass innards

Easley Does It

37. Jai ___
38. Math class, for short
41. Big initials on Mother's Day
42. Gives back, in a way
44. Passing partner's Texas transfer, e.g.
45. Catchall abbr.
46. Needle
47. Leaves out
48. Bridge writer Victor
49. Henry VIII's dynasty
52. NHL's Jaromir
53. USC foe
54. Distort, as the facts

56. Negating word
57. Off ___ (good result for a 11-across)
58. Copacabana city, informally
59. Mob turncoat

SECTION 3:
HARD
* * *

Across

1. Lunchbox fave, for short
4. Give the heave-ho
9. Nats, once
14. Metal in Montana's motto
15. What a train goes down
16. A bid often missed
17. Sooty overalls?
19. Call it a wrap
20. It comes before Smith in the ACBL Hall of Fame
21. Hinny's kin
23. "Lux et Veritas" school
24. Sermonize
27. Successful puzzlers' cries
29. Give two thumbs down
31. Eerie fruit?
36. VP between RMN and HHH
37. ACBL.org, e.g.
38. Frank
39. Utterance after uncovering a bad break
41. Accepted an evite, e.g. (abbr.)
43. Bonus, in adspeak
44. "Shake a leg!"
46. "The Time Machine" caste
48. Groovy
49. Picard, Riker and Worf plus Kirk, Spock, and Uhura?
51. Letters before Arizona or Maine
52. Ancient earth goddess
53. Erotic diarist Nin
55. Part of Nikki Sixx's band name
58. "We Do Our Part" org.
60. Two, for one
63. Opening with less than 12 HCPs, e.g.
65. Advice from a dermatologist?
68. Home ice?
69. Shelley, for one
70. "The Racer's Edge"
71. Hall of Famer who pitched his last game at age 59
72. It's just not done
73. Biblical possessive

Down

1. Some toys, briefly
2. Elan
3. Rocker who acted in "Pay It Forward"
4. Cap extensions
5. Follower of the nus?
6. Nittany Lions sch.
7. "A Streetcar Named Desire" director Kazan
8. Sics on
9. WSJ workers
10. Titillating novelty
11. "____ Vida" (Costa Rican greeting)
12. Lacking a paper trail, perhaps
13. End of a celebratory song
18. Eternally, in verse
22. Moment of truth
25. Suit-able number?
26. Spread, slangily
28. French intimate
29. Measure depth, in a way
30. Despise
32. End of a bridge saw

27

That Sounds About Right

33. Nut
34. Buenos ___
35. Harvests
40. Wonderland croquet ball
42. Many a prayer
45. Supermarket chain
47. Likely will
50. Escorts can be picked up here
54. Sale tag abbr.
55. Snippet
56. Capital of Latvia
57. Tangelo variety
59. Tragic Ethiopian princess
61. It's sometimes busted

62. Catch a glimpse of
64. Piggie
66. Smith and Jones movie, for short
67. Seeking, in personals

Across

1. Some e-mailed files, for short
5. Barracks furnishings
10. It's sometimes jumped
14. Do another hitch
15. "J'accuse" writer Zola
16. Minor opening?
17. Big earthenware jar
18. Capital 7,200 feet above sea level
19. It's mostly made of zinc
20. Gripping stuff?
22. Hawaiian staple
24. Take care of business
27. Creator of the Republican elephant
28. Lake in "Hairspray"
30. Vietnam's most common surname
32. 2012 Buffett Cup Challenge Match winner (abbr.)
33. Rear, slangily
34. How many a dare is done
38. Action sometimes done in bridge defense, and a hint to what's found in rows 3, 6, 10, and 13
42. "The Lion King" villains
43. "I'm onto you now!"
44. Mother's hermana
45. What "in" people are in
47. Pay one's card fees
49. Chinese for "water"
51. Its stock symbol is X
53. Mobile home?
55. Familiarly, it's word-for-word?
58. Cabo's peninsula
59. Tabu competitor
62. Just ___ on the map
63. Tag line?
64. Eagle's nest, e.g.
65. Salade niçoise ingredient
66. To be, in Latin
67. Gripper, of a sort
68. "Lawrence of Arabia", e.g.

Down

1. B.C., e.g.
2. A stet cancels it
3. Not reduced
4. Oscar winner as Lynn
5. Intoxicate
6. First name in the "Pulp Fiction" credits
7. "Delta of Venus" author
8. Alien visitor in "The Day the Earth Stood Still"
9. Mark of authenticity
10. President who remained a lifelong bachelor
11. Branches of study
12. Argumentative retort
13. ___ play
21. Big letters in outdoor gear
23. 12-14, sometimes
25. ___ even keel
26. Like granite
28. Hotfoot it
29. Road game

Breaking Up is Hard To Do

(crossword grid)

31. Pirate song start
33. "___ fan Tutte"
35. Like repressed feelings
36. Shallowest of the Great Lakes
37. Autocrat of old
39. Develop slowly
40. First name in the "Rocky" credits
41. "___ Gotta Have It" (1986 Spike Lee film)
46. Member of the Society of Friends
47. Fairness-in-hiring letters

48. Overturn
49. Subjects of many an exploration
50. Some pilgrims
52. Cornered, in a way
53. Guy with an Irish Rose
54. Future GP's exam
56. "Beloved" author Morrison
57. Opp. of legato, in music
60. Bauxite, e.g.
61. First name in the "My Big Fat Greek Wedding" credits

ACROSS

1. Trade barbs
5. Screw thread, e.g.
10. Throws a wrench into opps' bidding
14. Italian menu word
15. Tex-Mex menu word
16. The eyes have it?
17. Famous bridge player who had a penchant for quickly spreading the cards and walking away when he was dummy
19. _____-Roman (convention using a 2D opening)
20. "Mea culpa"
21. IAD letters
22. It sometimes gives pard a clue in choosing a lead
23. Divine name in showbiz
25. Olfactory offender
27. "Breaking Bad" broadcaster
29. 17-across once ended up dummy with David Burnstine of ___ sitting to his right
34. Recurring "Seinfeld" character from Pakistan
36. Chat room shorthand
37. Rita Hayworth title role of 1946
38. Amenhotep IVs sole deity
39. Bill of legend
42. Nice evening?
43. Some Zero Tolerance offenders, perhaps
45. Guitar, slangily
46. James with legendary pipes
47. Burnstine pondered over his decision and quickly slapped something down, causing 17-across to reflexively table the dummy and give away the ___
51. QVC rival
52. Orchestral pitch setter
53. Take the wrong way?
55. Apple on a desk, perhaps
58. Some choice words?
60. Penner of paeans
62. ___ crusher
63. This play has become known as the ___ Coup
66. Old buffalo hunters of the Great Plains
67. How sardines are often packed
68. "Hogwash!"
69. Unbeatable, slangily
70. Barely beat
71. Preoccupied with

DOWN

1. Save, for short
2. Prized
3. Flockhart hit with a recurring dancing baby hallucination
4. Yeshiva product
5. 6-0 break or every finesse being wrong, e.g.
6. Stab (abbr.)
7. Emit coherent light
8. "Same here!"
9. Charles Foster Kane's estate
10. It's often preemptive in competition
11. Saucony rival

29

Tales of Bridge

12. YMCA part
13. "Je ne ___ quoi"
18. The player asked "Any questions, pard?", in most bridge column layouts
24. Internet phenomenon, like the dancing baby
26. Internet address ending
27. One way to be taken
28. Arch opening?
30. The "f" in f-stop
31. It helps hold up many people's pants
32. Makes the cut?
33. Clear choice for the kitchen?
35. Made cards cashable, e.g.

40. Lugs
41. Shark Encounter site
44. Twin to one's twin, in short
48. Knuckle-headed move?
49. Coming or going, e.g.
50. ___ number on
54. Swedish girl of kiddie lit
55. Sporty Camaro
56. Detective portrayed by Lorre
57. Bidding system "Skid" Simon helped devise
59. Air condition?
61. Play to see if the opps' cards split 3-3, e.g.
64. Golfer who turned pro at 15
65. Density symbol, in physics

Across

1. Big bucks?
6. Norm (abbr.)
9. Canned crab?
14. Stew
15. It comes with status
16. "Ici on ___ français"
17. Bridge supporter
18. OAS member
19. Immune system agent
20. Shootout time, perhaps
21. Balkan people
23. Hero of Hinduism
24. Level below diamond in the ACBL
25. One-eyed "Futurama" character
26. Brit's indignant comment
27. Canonized mlles.
28. Tenochtitlán dweller
29. Sloughs
30. It might lead to a split
32. It means "water" overseas
34. Words after a holdup
37. Cravat's cousins
41. USA, in the inaugural Buffett Cup
42. Thanksgiving mo. in Canada
45. Elimination rhyme's start
46. Stalker of a 49-across, perhaps
47. Beatnik's acknowledgment
49. Quarry of a 46-across, perhaps
50. 1-, 4-, 6- , 8-, 10- and 13-down's place
55. Put on a coat?
56. King's take, perhaps
58. 1-, 4-, 6- , 8-, 10- and 13-down's place
63. Like JFK
64. Often heard pick-up line
65. Uncle Remus appellation
66. Rick of "Disco Duck" fame
67. Musician's better half?
68. Lyrical works

Down

1. Scoring for teams, e.g.
2. Additionally
3. Iris part
4. Source of many 1-down
5. One of Beethoven's nine (abbr.)
6. Knockout or strip, e.g.
7. Tank top?
8. Balancing and reopening, e.g.
9. Make a call (for)
10. Calculated 7C, perhaps
11. Clothes line?
12. Supremely macho
13. Many bids in the Ultimate Club system
21. Partial quality
22. He and Helena played a couple in "Les Miserables"
31. Nile reptile
33. Milk, in a way
34. Balance, e.g.
35. Shortened preposition
36. Break Zero Tolerance, as with one's pard
38. Published
39. Female in la familia

30

It's Where It's At

40. Defeat
42. Texter's WTF alternative
43. Amigo of Fidel
44. Naughty-sounding flyer
47. Fed. credentials
48. Film about the Statue of Liberty?
51. Cambodian dough
52. Like Brahms's Piano Trio No. 1
53. Offerer of support?
54. Cause for some to bend over backwards
55. Window shopper's purchase?

57. Dummy's seat, perhaps
58. Balance, e.g.
59. Perishable wear
60. Inc., abroad
61. End in 1S, perhaps, as an auction
62. Rx writers

Across

1. Laid low
4. Clay being of Jewish lore
9. Diminutive dogs, for short
14. It includes mayo
15. Lone Star State landmark
16. Lifting device
17. Part 1 of a question asked to 41-across
20. The "A" in A.D.
21. Gryffindor's emblem
22. Spot for a cat nap, often
23. 1958 Chevalier musical
27. Ethan of literature
29. Part 2 of the question
33. Feminine palindrome
36. The "S" in R.S.V.P.
37. Slashed
40. Really tiny
41. Subject of this puzzle
44. Memo abbr.
45. Remove from a hold
46. Goal-oriented Hamm
47. Sought to win
49. Part 3 of the question
51. Mountain nymph of Greek myth
54. Mex. miss
55. Matching pair designation
57. Behind-the-scenes view?
59. Norah's father
63. Answer given by 41-across (while pointing to her partner, Charles Goren)
68. Make a somnolent sound
69. Sturdy string
70. Place for an X
71. Naval acronym
72. In a class of one's own
73. "The Big Easy" of golf

Down

1. "Funny!" or "Funny... not!"
2. Privy to
3. -100, e.g.
4. D.C. auditing agency
5. Root word?
6. UNLV part
7. Oscar-winning actor Jannings
8. Recurring theme
9. Justin Lall as a teen, e.g.
10. Nondiscrimination letters
11. Sat out, perhaps
12. It is, in Spain
13. Red card, e.g.
18. Thing in a roundup
19. Pro
24. "Victory is mine!"
25. Big name in infomercial knives
26. "The show is starting!"
28. Seriously hurt
29. "Balderdash!"
30. Lead astray
31. More quickly than desired
32. Speak in Spanish?
34. Bustling
35. "... or I'll eat ___!"
38. Needs braces?
39. Respected villager
42. Cabinet dept. created in 1977
43. Blue note?

48. Jazz legend Gordon
50. Transmission setting
52. Bearer of pairs
53. "Purgatorio" writer
55. Greeting for a villain
56. Passport fig.
58. Caterwaul
60. (sigh)
61. Perfumery unit
62. They're valuable in GNTs
64. Influential DC lobby
65. Nintendo debut of 2006
66. Red army member?
67. Gloater's shout

Across

1. A NT contract at heart, often
5. Dust-up
9. Auction actions
13. Model from Mogadishu
14. "A line is ___ that went for a walk": Klee
15. Transgress Zero Tolerance, perhaps
16. Premium price
18. Gather feedback
19. Man "against whom no one ever makes a wrong bid or play"
21. "Give it ___!"
22. Bumbler
23. Grassland grazer
26. Held up, maybe
27. "A man with an unnaturally sour disposition"
31. Etc. kin
32. "___ it when none of my finesses work!"
33. Woman "who tends to mix up jacks and kings but always somehow finds the killing play by mistake"

38. Like a windmill
39. "Well, Did You ___?"
40. Man "who knows that the Fates will conspire against him whatever he does"
43. Wallop
47. 100 Acre Wood youngster
48. Dr. Zaius, e.g.
49. "The Rights of Man" author
50. Bridge writer whose club 19-, 27-, 33-, and 50-across belong to
54. Lock horns
57. "Not a prob!"
58. It has four hands
59. Big Red rivals
60. "NYPD Blue" actor Morales
61. Jittery
62. Stops up
63. Triangular muscle, briefly

Down

1. Mass, for one
2. Egyptian Sun God
3. It's not hard to swallow
4. Ultimate purpose
5. Chew the fat
6. In a slothful way
7. One in a mare's nest?
8. '60s sitcom set at Fort Courage
9. ___ Team

10. It's not free of charge
11. Minor application
12. Babe's digs
15. "Birth of a Nation" director
17. 10, at times (abbr.)
20. Fed. of Persian Gulf states
23. Island north of New Guinea
24. Insignificant details
25. Salt Lake City collegian

32

At the Club

27. Sporty VW model
28. "Diff'rent Strokes" actress Charlotte
29. Former U.S. Vice President Barkley
30. Balancer, perhaps (abbr.)
31. Won over
33. Clinic name of fame
34. Digging
35. Book after Ezr.
36. Egg (prefix)
37. Middle X, perhaps
38. TiVo forerunner
41. Pro at balancing

42. Hankered
43. Blew a gasket
44. Facilitate communication
45. "OMG!"
46. Digs
49. Pricer's word
50. Last word in a Faulkner title
51. Caffeine-laden nut
52. Skinny-dip
53. Pitch
54. Half a sawbuck
55. Cone's partner
56. Wisecrack

Across

1. Meddler
6. Features of a 2C opener, often
10. Letters of invitation?
14. Bagel, topologically
15. Bridge legend Spingold
16. Legendary
17. Correct a well-known puppet?
20. Bacon measure
21. Baffled inquiries
22. After, in Arles
23. Golden rule word
25. Have chutzpah
27. Being okay with bottoms?
32. "The Planets" composer
33. Leave out
34. "Good Grips" kitchenware brand
36. Still having a shot to win
37. Action preceding an endplay
39. Analogist's words
40. Slangy word of indifference
41. Gazillions
42. Finished first, as in a Bermuda Bowl
43. "Uh, duh, I guess I changed me mind"?
47. "As if!"
48. Othello's adversary
49. Garlicky spread
52. Save against a game, for short
53. Movie-rating org.
57. Two judges in divorce court?
61. Boring result
62. First name in both bridge and moviedom
63. Action for losers
64. Old Testament twin
65. Ashram activity
66. Brash

Down

1. Violins and cellos (abbr.)
2. Coward of note
3. Pacific predator
4. "I object!", e.g.
5. Parapsychology term
6. Slangy segue
7. Jazz devotees
8. Addis Ababa's land (abbr.)
9. Poker option
10. Make a double in the passout seat, e.g.
11. Cowpoke's poker
12. Kudzu, for one
13. Matchpoints results (abbr.)
18. Intergalactic bounty hunter Boba ___
19. Diamond number
24. "Wayne's World" cry
25. Jane in "G.I. Jane"
26. Give it ___ (swing hard)
27. Established districts
28. Root of diplomacy
29. Michaels of "Saturday Night Live"
30. ___ del Sol, Spain
31. Heap kudos on
32. One of LBJ's beagles
35. Alley of fame

33

A Turn of Phrase 2

37. Ocular inflammation
38. Legal misdeed
39. Staying up state?
41. Sphere of influence
42. URL ender
44. Social sphere
45. It might keep one up
46. By the unit
49. Court legend
50. NASDAQ events
51. Big earthenware jar
52. 5-0 split, e.g.
54. 51-downs, e.g.

55. Story trajectories
56. Lacking color
58. Trinket
59. Texter's qualifying letters
60. Special ___

ACROSS

1. Current event?
6. Bad press
10. Not even close
14. It might bring back memories
15. "Doctor Zhivago" heroine
16. Gluten-free grain
17. Usually a tricky problem
19. TV neigh-sayer?
20. Athos, to Aramis
21. Crews' directors
22. Wild West show prop
23. Fail (with "go")
24. Magilla Gorilla, for one
25. Intimidate
27. Common club game
31. Tacked on
34. Pinion's partner
35. Boston hockey legend
36. Opening salvo
37. Gemstones from Australia
39. Booty
40. It may be smoked at certain bars
41. Two-cup units?
42. Concerto finale, often
43. Often a weak opener
47. Casting choice?
48. Leaves in hot water?
49. Airline that Howard Hughes bought in '39
52. Cartographer's creation
54. Record company
56. Bird by the beach
57. Green-blue hue
58. Jill and Bobby Levin, e.g.
60. Playpen plaint
61. Sci-fi sights
62. Go back on one's word?
63. Guess, as after a four-level preempt
64. Nick's cousin
65. Ravens' havens

DOWN

1. Pops
2. A feather in one's cap
3. Fess up to
4. Volcano feature
5. Trump king, often
6. Went from solid to liquid, e.g.
7. Feeble
8. Piece offering
9. Boastful Round Table knight
10. Big name in high fashion
11. Ravens' reset, of a sort
12. Corn-y team?
13. Edit menu command
18. Bridge convention useful after Blackwood intereference
22. Hang around in the shadows
26. Fundamentals
27. Retirement spot?
28. Understand
29. Mortarboard tosser
30. Deducer's word
31. Amber quaffs
32. ____ Finesse
33. Renowned exile
37. Roughly
38. One of the 33-down's priors

34

Repeat Business

39. xx, sometimes
41. Seeks change?
42. They shun quiche, supposedly
44. Site of some fingerprinting, of a sort
45. If all goes according to plan
46. Skillful feat
49. High level transfer?
50. Take by force
51. Chilean range
52. Do-re-mi dispensers (abbr.)
53. Milk dispenser
55. Cellular transmitter

58. Carding convention from xxx
59. Hotness

Across

1. Where one might get a date
5. Most extreme degree
8. These, overseas
13. Fille's friend
14. Horror film splatters, e.g.
15. Squirreled-away things
16. Like many a Bermuda Bowl kibitzer
17. Bidding system popular in Britain
18. Card involved in a squeeze
19. Good judge of a bridge hand?
22. Bid 1C, e.g.
23. Leslie Caron film of 1953
24. Good judge of a bridge hand?
32. Harper of writing
33. Axis bigwig
34. Not a soul
35. Descendants of Ishmael
38. The Muses' domain
41. Capacious cask
42. Good judge of a bridge hand?
47. "Look ___!"
48. Defeat by 50 IMPs, e.g.
49. Place 19-, 24-, 42-across were once found (when not playing a bridge hand)
56. Coming from the heart?
57. Sphere of specialty
58. Middle Eastern money
60. Sylvester's quarry
61. On its way
62. Family moniker
63. Get home safely, perhaps
64. General mentioned on menus
65. Fifth Avenue landmark

Down

1. Best possible result for both sides
2. Key of Beethoven's Seventh (abbr.)
3. Slimming option, for short
4. System
5. "I'm afraid that's quite impossible"
6. Drop ___ (moon)
7. Hot spot?
8. Grand Life Master, e.g.
9. "Mighty Aphrodite" actress
10. Kite eater in "Peanuts"
11. Put ___ act
12. 2003 retirees (abbr.)
14. Watch experts in astonishment, as many a Bermuda Bowl kibitzer
15. Room at the top?
20. Where Will Shortz is "the Puzzle Master" (abbr.)
21. ___-Blo (fuse brand)
24. Picnic staple
25. Atmospheric prefix
26. Best Actress Patricia
27. A bit cracked
28. In times past
29. "It wasn't me!"
30. Albatross, e.g.
31. Occupancy fee

35

Judgment Call

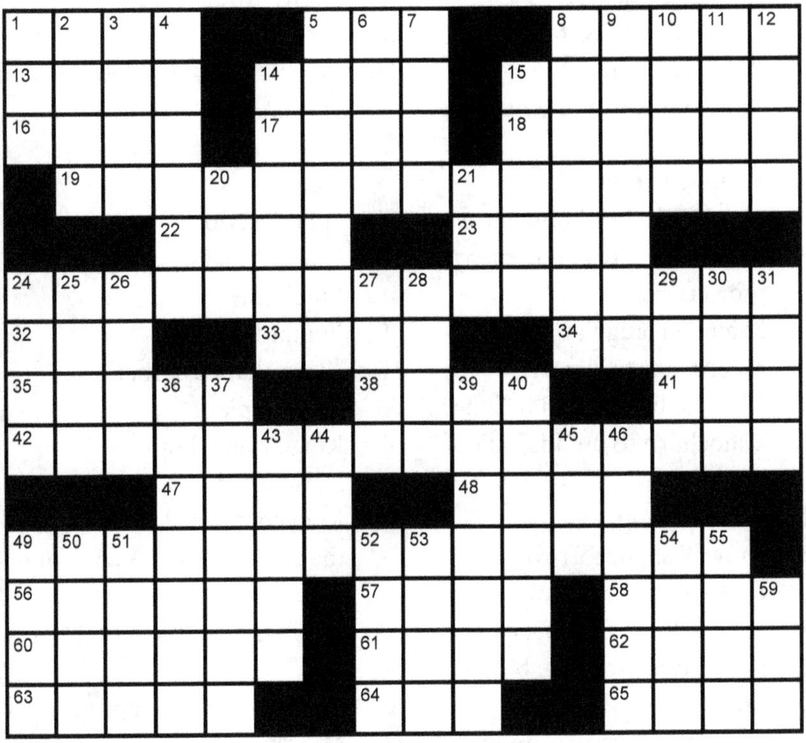

36. Jumped right to grand slam after partner opened 1D, e.g.
37. Place in a place
39. Subject of Hamman's Rule, briefly
40. Transport on treads
43. In spades
44. Sea, overseas
45. Status chaser?
46. Some reversals
49. Ink, slangily
50. React to a kneeslapper
51. Chunk of the Elba palindrome
52. Half of half of all bridge tables
53. GI rations
54. Pirate-hunting group (abbr.)
55. Huddle for ages, deciding what to bid
59. UNLV part

Across

1. Armrest, of a sort
6. Lily that's Utah's state flower
10. BMOCs, often
13. "Stupid me, I should have led your suit!"
14. Wrap selection
15. The ACBL's head honcho, e.g.
16. Some of The Donald's many projects
18. Kramden laugh syllable
19. MacArthur trademark
20. "I'll beat him so bad he'll need a shoehorn to put his hat on" boaster
21. Nincompoop
23. Show of sham sorrow
26. Heavy duty?
27. White House Cabinet dept.
28. Surmise, as from the bidding
30. Rig
32. He played with Lew on the 1985 Bermuda Bowl-winning team
36. Spike in production?

37. Shower room sight
40. Vote (for)
41. "WKRP" costar of Gordon and Howard
43. Simpson who's a fan of crosswords
44. Spherical dos
46. Club, of a sort
48. Pupil's site
49. Frankfurters' kin
55. "Zero chance of that!"
56. NBC staple
57. King Priam's home
59. Naval Acad. grad
60. Knockout punch, and a hint to the starts of 16-, 23-, 37-, and 49-across
63. Jack Ryan's employer (abbr.)
64. _____ deep
65. Bridge Bulletin wrap-up
66. Mrs. Michael Corleone
67. Request to a barkeep
68. Staggers

Down

1. Internet standard for e-mail (abbr.)
2. Line at a karaoke bar
3. Pain reliever selection
4. Disbelieving demand
5. Annual IMF calculation
6. 2005 horror film sequel
7. Before, to Byron
8. Corsage favorite
9. At the scene itself
10. Soft vowel sound

11. Run again, as the final "Cheers" episode
12. Puts into suits, e.g.
14. "It's a deal!"
17. Art colony of the Southwest
22. Chicago exchange, for short
24. Keep in check
25. Logical proposition
28. Bugged by a bug
29. "The Matrix" hero
30. Frat rooms, often

36

Many, in Marseilles?

31. Canadian interjections
33. Close match, like many Spingold finals
34. NASDAQ debut
35. The P of VPs
38. Eliot Ness raided his speakeasies
39. Renowned 1939 film setting
42. "Now ___ expert, but..."
45. Source of a legendary leaf
47. Pain reliever selection
48. Capri, e.g.
49. Sweater style

50. Alexander the Great conquered it
51. Lamb product
52. Play ___ card (follow low)
53. Reverse the effects of
54. L.A. locale
58. Slangy assents
61. Hagen of "Reversal of Fortune"
62. Boxer's warning

ACROSS

1. Letter that sounds regretful
4. Improve, as one's declarer play skills
8. Put in stitches
12. Mo. for fools
13. Big ape, for short
15. Drezna denials
16. Copacabana setting
17. Metric prefix
18. On the whole
19. Leading tennis player/celebrity of old, known as one of the "Spice Girls of Tennis"
22. Pierre's st.
23. Payment to many a post-doc
25. Leading gymnast of the 1972 Olympics
30. Users of the dark side
31. Strong alkali
32. First in a historical trio
33. Punitive
34. Leading lady of "Black Swan" and "Forgetting Sarah Marshall"

37. Central character in David Bird's bridge writings
40. Joie de vivre
41. Draft lottery org.
44. Stocking stuffers?
45. Leading singer of old who Orson Welles called "the most exciting woman in the world"
48. Airplane thrusters
50. Classic Langston Hughes poem
51. Source of many a good lead, and what 19-, 25-, 34-, and 45-across all contain
56. Make a lousy match
57. Bucolic spots
58. Hemming sounds
59. Slow, on a score
60. Man with a respected thumb
61. It has no losers
62. In ___ (existing)
63. Sign away
64. NBC inits. since 1975

DOWN

1. Sunscreen, of a sort
2. Thin and fragile
3. Period when man really forged ahead?
4. Sell at a pawnshop
5. Little dipper?
6. Half a sitcom send-off
7. ___'acte
8. Bridge Bulletin event abridgments, e.g.
9. Let stand, as a double

10. Site of a 2013 52-down
11. Couture monogram
14. Infomercial cutter
15. Supermodel Taylor
20. Letters on a rap sheet
21. "Addams Family" cousin
24. UPS rival
26. Put in stitches?
27. "Texas tea"
28. Genetics abbr.
29. One of a nursery rhyme trio

Leaders of the Pack

33. First word of a tropical drink
34. Exactly the right word
35. Last, for short
36. "No way"
37. Part of ANC
38. Johnny and the Moondogs, later
39. Laments, as a misplayed hand
41. Idle times
42. Kick down a door
43. Newsman John
45. Country in 37-down (abbr.)
46. Parenthetical comment
47. Blood, so to speak
49. Defensive signal, often
52. ACBL event
53. Fox premiere of 2009
54. Range rover?
55. Bony prefix
56. Cavs on a scoreboard

Across

1. One pursued by Azrael
6. Singer on the big screen
10. Football legend Graham
14. One or more in xxx, often
15. "Law & Order: SVU" actor
16. Skip levels, e.g.
17. Mystified
18. "Liquor is quicker" poet
19. Cold-blooded killers
20. Singletons pulling their weight?
23. He often batted after Babe
24. Call to dummy at the end of some hands
25. Film in which Will Ferrell says "Good news-I saw a dog today!"
28. Unexpected ruff, at times?
33. Indonesian tongue
34. Challenger to DDE
35. The "kid" in "Here's looking at you, kid"
36. Prefix meaning "within"
37. "No problemo!"
39. Defender, about half the time
40. It may be ad hoc (abbr.)
41. Manny's Pale ___ (Seattle microbrew)
42. They get people into jams
43. Director, sometimes?
47. Little power sources
48. Sounds of sympathy
49. Symbol of mightiness
50. "Did I win that in hand or in dummy?", e.g.?
57. Treat often disassembled before consumption
59. Charlotte and Norma
60. Starting word of a "Willy Wonka" song
61. Racy rumors
62. Doing what needs to be done
63. Made decisions in diamonds
64. Pizzazz
65. Particle flux density symbols
66. Rival of Edison

Down

1. Hero's accompanier, perhaps
2. Marquand's Mr.
3. SALT signatory
4. Be a real stinker
5. Achilles' heel
6. Latin tongue
7. Edible South American tubers
8. Paraphrased, perhaps
9. "Sounds about right"
10. One of Snoopy's brothers
11. Arrange into a checkered pattern, e.g.
12. Spy's device
13. Jobs for SEALs
21. Postal creed conjunction
22. Memo letters
26. Complex individual?
27. Places people rush to get into
28. Vegetable oil source
29. Target of many fakes
30. Watts in pictures
31. Switch-hit?
32. Title for Sulu on "Star Trek" (abbr.)

Bridge on the Mind 2

33. Hub
37. It brings in the bucks
38. The Last Frontier folks
42. Invites
44. Miss Piggy query
45. Tilts
46. OPEC member
51. Stone's partner of note
52. Liner of note, briefly
53. "The Official Encyclopedia of Bridge", e.g.
54. Measure of many a swing (abbr.)
55. German auto export
56. Big zero
57. Low-high meaning, often
58. Fjord-like body

ACROSS

1. Site of the Taj Mahal
5. Exclusion-principle formulator
10. Champagne designation
14. Big name in movie theaters
15. Exposed
16. Vintners' prefix
17. Spatter cone's output
18. Disciplinary
19. Dollar's competition
20. Detective who analyzed bridge score pads in "Cards on the Table"
23. Total, e.g.
24. Some Russian imports
26. Is down with
27. Contract
31. The Renaissance, e.g.
32. Metaphorical light bulb
34. "Director!", e.g.
35. "... and ___ it again!"
36. Operative who dealt an enemy a 31-point hand
39. Old gold coin of Europe
42. Aristotle's H
43. Open, in a way
47. Ancient Turkish landfall
49. Words spoken with glass raised
50. Downed Russian orbiter
51. Imps
55. Barracks VIP
56. World-traveler whose "only pastime was reading the papers and playing whist"
59. "Buzz off!"
61. Romero who played The Joker
62. Huck Finn's ride
65. Handyman's asset
66. Handy
67. It's quite a stretch
68. With 70-across, tragic heroine and bridge player in "The House of Mirth"
69. Responded to a cattle call?
70. See 68-across

DOWN

1. Nothing but
2. "Be my guest"
3. Often-unrecognized bid
4. Clued in
5. Democratic doctrine
6. "Clan of the Cave Bear" author
7. Alternative-media mag
8. Jump, as to game
9. "Count me in!"
10. It often travels with a traveller
11. Erred in ruffing in, perhaps
12. Gymnast's getup
13. Lean-___
21. Jazz man
22. Particle in a cloud chamber
23. Life energy, in the East
25. ___ Tome and Principe
28. Clarified butter used in India
29. Brigde party thrower
30. Horn of plenty?
33. Slightly cracked
35. SSN, e.g.
37. Asteroids source
38. Crackers

Written in the Cards

39. Stop up
40. Alleged mentalist Geller
41. Efficient way to work?
44. Hypothetical supercontinent
45. Key to an exit?
46. In a '64 song it's "really lookin' fine"
48. After-bath application
49. Bridge expert who paired with Edgar
52. Take care of
53. Tokyo-based electronics company
54. Words after make or close
57. Part of HRE
58. Take while still possible, as an ace
59. Cardinal letters
60. ___ polloi
63. Pro
64. Letters on many a Wile E. Coyote contraption

SECTION 4:
CHALLENGING

****

Across

1. Spoke like Don Corleone
7. More, in a score
10. Lettuce variety
14. Become breathless?
15. Access points
16. Prime rating
17. Clears for takeoff?
18. Many a bridge player
20. Standard fare for magicians
22. Special follower
23. Initials in old Europe
24. Vintner's prefix
25. "With Reagan" memoir writer
28. Signaling option
33. Punch line?
36. Lincoln's in-laws
37. Newbery Medal winner Lowry
38. Titillate
40. Like Omaha, for example
42. Shih ___

43. Daunted
46. Staples staples, for short
47. Be in control
51. The Corleones, e.g.
52. Lille lily
55. Eastern discipline
57. They may be fluid (abbr.)
58. Offensive threat
62. Pressure applicator, and a hint to six squares in this puzzle
65. New Jersey mountain range
66. GM or MG, e.g.
67. "Rocky" film with Clubber Lang
68. Sees through
69. Words of cheer?
70. Onetime Bowie collaborator
71. "Bridge for Dummies" author

Down

1. X, for one
2. An ___ grind
3. Corleone portrayer
4. Corleone portrayer
5. TVA output
6. Escritoire, for one
7. Notable Earl Grey drinker
8. IRS data
9. One of the majors
10. Nice nice
11. Having big-time problems
12. It has a head but no shoulders
13. Expose to danger, in a way
19. Brought into play
21. NABC spot

26. Pirate's booty? (abbr.)
27. Minuteman's home?
29. Skid row woe, for short
30. John of mystery
31. Hearty adjective?
32. IRS data
33. What comes out of a 35-down
34. Avgolemono pasta
35. Producer of 33-downs
39. Govt. grader
40. Match
41. Driver's license, e.g. (abbr.)
43. Pen up
44. Causes of excitement in the NIT

Under Pressure

45. Lark
48. "A man may learn wisdom
    even from ___" (Aristophanes)
49. Tin ___
50. Hit hard, as brakes
53. "Ain't gonna happen!"
54. Dividing membranes
55. Winter Palace VIP
56. Water color
59. French composer Satie
60. Pathfinder org.
61. Site for some T-bones
63. Dawn deity
64. Jazzercise, informally

Across

1. Convention: respond 3C to a 1NT opening
7. Spanish 101 word
11. Davis' realm (abbr.)
14. Pamplona shout
15. Take out
16. Go to a minor, perhaps
17. "Fat chance of that!"
18. Convention: open 2NT
20. Plains peoples
22. NZ makeup
23. Convention: respond 3C to a 1S opening
26. Place for many a grilling, briefly
28. "So that's your game, eh?"
29. Spanish 101 word
30. "À la Recherche du Temps Perdu" author
31. Go to a minor, perhaps
33. Class that's for kicks?
35. Convention: respond 3H to a 1NT opening
40. Full of baloney
41. Strategic WWI river
43. Ravel opus
45. Cable company acquired by AT&T
48. Common word on Brazilian maps
49. French city with a 1598 edict
50. Convention: open 1D
52. Old World tongue
53. "Do the Right Thing" actor
54. Convention: bid 4D after 1C-1H-3H
57. "Choose a lead already!"
61. The last word?
62. Give the finger to?
63. Made like Spade
64. Gin grain
65. Greenery on trees
66. Common result, and what the clues for 1-, 18-, 23-, 35-, 50-, and 54-across are

Down

1. Geometric suffix
2. "Sweet Talkin' Woman" grp.
3. Legal term
4. First of an author's set
5. Cosmo's chum
6. Transplants
7. He developed a bidding system with Alfred
8. They're married in Mex.
9. Voldemort's real first name
10. SFPD advisory
11. Baked desserts
12. Naturally bright?
13. Teen sensation?
19. Deliquesce
21. Obstruction, of a sort
23. xx, sometimes
24. Dope, slangily
25. Score in a pointless game
26. Muffin stuffin'
27. Many BBO players
30. Jibber-jabber
32. August
34. Art, today?

36. Protected, in a way
37. Some high-end cameras, for short
38. North Carolina's motto starter
39. Duff
42. 1986 Rookie of the Year Welland
43. Nobleman's domain
44. Pick-up-able, e.g.
46. Beckon
47. Green, as trees
49. Suit combination adage ender
50. Bona ___ (good faith)
51. "___ but when"

53. Green lights, as at NASA
55. Stat in a pool
56. Tic-tac-toe winner
58. Mo lead-in
59. J.E.B. Stuart, for one
60. Pindar piece

Across

1. Oranjestad's land
6. (fizzle)
10. ABA affiliate
14. Middle name in mystery fiction
15. Makeup of some beehives
16. Many a Chulalongkorn Day celebrant
17. Bridge "maxim" coined by Milton Shattner, starting at 29-across
19. Flag at a night session
20. "Isaac's Storm" author Larson
21. First name in spy fiction
22. All in a lather?
24. Team with a mascot named Uga, familiarly
26. Band with a lightning bolt in its logo
27. Medium for some sculptors (abbr.)
29. "Maxim", part 1
34. Card discard
36. Geller feller
37. ___ uproar
38. Après-midi follower
39. Was ready for the heat (abbr.)
41. "99 Luftballons" band
42. Encouragement starter
43. It sits east on some faces
44. Contract bridge?
45. "Maxim", part 2
49. ABA members
50. Head-smacking utterances
51. Selassie disciple, informally
53. Insurer of the Titanic
56. Blue card's signal, sometimes (abbr.)
57. Smacking sound
60. Harmonize
61. "Maxim", part 3
64. Bailiwick
65. "Revenge of the Nerds" bully
66. Nephritic
67. See if a suit splits 3-3, perhaps
68. Bolshevik's bane
69. One of Billy's partners on the Aces

Down

1. Part of a plot?
2. Reaction to a grand slam, sometimes
3. Source of many a 10-down lead
4. Cake highlighted in a "Seinfeld" episode
5. First name in folk rock
6. Musical passage
7. Horned deity
8. Chick-___-A
9. "Ooh la la!"
10. See 3-down
11. He won a GNT and NAP with his wife Jan
12. Ditch one's protector, e.g.
13. Bent a convention, perhaps
18. (I concede)
23. Paean in verse
25. Grp. with a panda logo
26. Cutting-edge brand?
27. Very, in scores

42

Well, Duh!

28. Stigmas
30. Film with a lot of raw footage?
31. 56-across' meaning, perhaps
32. Title of familial fondness
33. Summertime swarm
35. One who rarely tries for grand slam, perhaps
39. Most memorable moment
40. Feels rocky
44. FAQ bit
46. Affirmative action?
47. Mini-Me portrayer of "Austin Powers"
48. Malt-drying oven

52. It might suit you
53. GRE's cousin
54. Orpheus's instrument
55. Aces, sometimes
56. First name in bakery products
58. Drupe rich in antioxidants
59. "The Black Pearl"
62. Some HDTVs
63. Dominion until 1806 (abbr.)

Across

1. Blitzer's goal
5. Like some boards and hands
9. Site of a 1969 "miracle"
13. First course of action
15. Per
16. Bridge site
17. Los Aztecas worshipped it
18. Minuscule contribution
19. Intro drawing class
20. Femme fatale of 1992, 2004, and 2012
22. "The Blind Assassin" novelist
24. 1940s baseball great Buck
25. Repentant ones
26. E.T. from Melmac
28. Less like a 31-across
30. Pink elephant sighter, perhaps
31. See 28-across
34. Jewel box contents, sometimes
36. Attacks
37. Popular system literally appearing an appropriate number of times in this puzzle
38. Get slick, in a way
42. Accepted, say (abbr.)
44. "Constant Craving" singer
45. Former ring king
48. Prophecy deliverer
50. "V for Vendetta" lead
51. Ph.D.'s next position, often
53. Something worth its weight in gold?
56. False start?
57. One of 45-across's strengths
60. Groucho-esque look
61. Kvetch
63. Hoopster who dubbed himself "The Big Aristotle"
64. Ireland's nickname
65. Fashionista's read
66. Urbane
67. Jet-setters' jets, once (abbr.)
68. Pass out at the table?
69. ___-dieu

Down

1. Blueprint datum, for short
2. Ristorante's "in the style of"
3. Rejects
4. Prominent
5. XX carrier
6. Gone belly up?
7. Make a scene?
8. Show place
9. Napster creator Fanning
10. NBC drama with a villain named Sylar
11. Barcelona bull
12. In the thick of
14. Natural soother
21. Captive in a box, sometimes
23. Doughnut, geometrically
25. Shoe company named after a bball phrase
26. Louisville Slugger material
27. Mauna ___
29. Electrifying letters?
32. Pothole patch
33. "Very weird..."
35. It's often torn in soccer (abbr.)

Use the Force

37. Another stage name for Makaveli
39. Very wide, in a way
40. French one
41. Tour group? (abbr.)
43. Sped, like a dragster
44. Bingo kin
45. Half of an incomparable mixture
46. Ditching target, often
47. Discoverer's words
49. Model train giant
52. Changes colors
54. Classic Pontiac muscle cars

55. Come clean
57. F.D.R.'s pooch
58. First name in raga
59. Bauhaus school teacher
62. Fútbol yell

Across

1. Physicist with a gas law named after him
6. Brief rule?
9. Longtime first name in New York Times bridge columns
13. Buck of baseball's Negro Leagues
14. Wine opener?
15. Peacekeeping org. since 1949
16. Passed out, in a way
17. Player of many NFL games
18. Queen's nickname
19. Ace
22. "Charles in Charge" star
23. Night sticks?
24. Ace
29. Specter of politics
30. Glowing discovery of 1898
31. Conned
34. Tournament level
35. "M*A*S*H" role
37. Bar for a guitar
38. Cruciverbalist's dir.
39. Certain royal in 27-down
40. Barely flowed
41. Ace
44. 1980's Sandinista leader
47. Pueblo cooking vessel
48. Ace
52. Scores
53. Skye, e.g.
54. NASA gear
57. London gallery
58. Sensation
59. Minuscule, informally
60. Checker, of sorts
61. Relations
62. Palms yielding starch

Down

1. Weightlifter's pride, slangily
2. Half and half?
3. "You betcha!"
4. Dogpatch denizen
5. Loop looper
6. Stigma of fiction
7. ___'acte
8. Enforcer of a speed limit
9. Mainstay
10. Musical syllables
11. Failed spectacularly
12. High times?
14. "Unreal!"
20. Belittle, as yo' mama
21. Either director of "The Ladykillers"
24. "Toodle-oo!"
25. Meckwell opener?
26. Pirate for short, e.g.
27. See 39-across
28. School lobby org.
31. Six-Day War battleground
32. Bid 3NT, at times
33. Bridges of "Diff'rent Strokes"
35. Threw caution to the wind
36. "What happened then?"
37. Great Barrier Reef locale
39. Saucy name?
40. Does a favor for
41. _____ minor
42. Lackey
43. Rivendell resident

44. Egg-shaped
45. 2S response, sometimes
46. Liquid paper?
49. Wine city of Italy
50. "Havana" star
51. Bean-sprouts bean
55. Metric prefix
56. Detmer and Law

ACROSS

1. Star of multiple video games
6. Like SAYC
11. Palindromic plus-size supermodel
14. A sweet finish
15. Last name in the Roberts court
16. It comes before one
17. Capital whose name means "place of the gods"
18. "Air Music" composer Ned
19. Pipsqueak
20. Diva's desire
22. Fixture in many a basement
24. "...___ quit!"
25. Shortage
26. Frequent problem in playing/defending a hand
32. Jump to game, e.g.
33. Sashimi serving
34. Jane Austin heroine
35. Card that often provides 26-across
37. 39-down, e.g.
41. HS class with a lot of unknowns
42. Like a gambling 3NT long suit, typically
43. Features that help with 26-across (this puzzle has four)
49. Name from a Hebrew word for "God is with us"
50. Regulus's constellation
51. Jibber-jabber
52. They're employed by many a spy
58. Huey, Dewey, and Louie, e.g.
59. Over one's head
61. First name in the Roberts court
62. Cambodian currency, and a prominent figure in Canadian history
63. Ends of the earth?
64. As ___ resort
65. Stock keeping unit?
66. Common contraction
67. Columbus's hometown

DOWN

1. Jannings and Zatopek
2. Chip choice
3. Experiment
4. Classic detergent brand
5. Sun Salutation, e.g.
6. Inner-city area
7. Mucho
8. Salutation of a sort
9. Suburban add-on?
10. Work against
11. Nobelist Fermi
12. First word in a Ewan McGregor feature
13. Renoir contemporary
21. Ernst contemporary
23. Non alternative?
25. Meckwell, e.g.
26. Number in a Tuscany 58-across
27. Butter, of sorts

45

Hand to Hand Combat

1	2	3	4	5		6	7	8	9	10		11	12	13

(crossword grid)

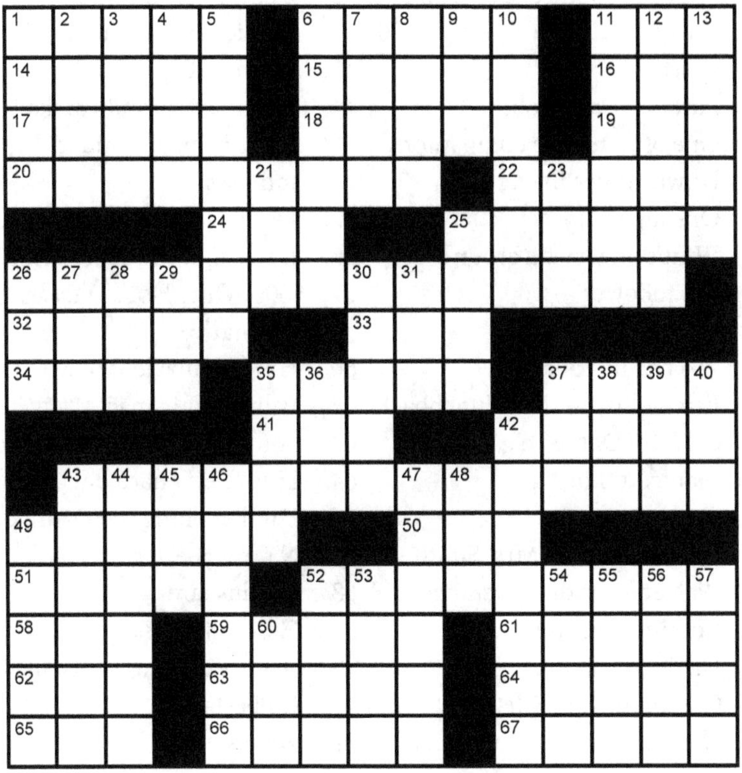

28. Sight-see?
29. Advisers to the POTUS
30. 20-21, e.g.
31. Albeit, briefly
35. Word to the POTUS
36. Done to death
37. Pro
38. "When you're as great as I am, it's hard to be humble" speaker
39. 37-across, e.g.
40. Inc. workers
42. Primitive period
43. Containing more of a granola grain

44. Incalculable, as wealth
45. Mardi Gras, e.g. (abbr.)
46. Celestial being
47. Heir to the throne, e.g.
48. Name clarifier
49. Hit from "West Side Story"
52. Unbeatable, as in a partial
53. Hot spot?
54. Woody, e.g.
55. Intended
56. Belgian painter James
57. Thai appetizer often served with peanut sauce
60. It's a wrap

Across

1. Start of a toon's exclamation
6. Nasty shock (like finding a 5-0 split)
10. Part of a frame job?
14. One of Artemis's companions
15. Down-under flock
16. One logged in
17. Whips one's head around
19. Pro follower
20. CPR pros
21. "To be," in Tours
22. Esmeralda in "The Hunchback of Notre Dame," e.g.
23. Manicotti kin
25. Grow tiresome
27. Emulates Mr. & Mrs. Smith
31. Walker of bridge teachings
34. Roaring Twenties, e.g.
35. Habit, to some
37. Common texting letters
38. One-two punch, so to speak
42. Serve up a whopper?
43. Conv. used in some interference situations
45. Panama, e.g.
46. Like many brandy casks
48. It has its pluses and its minuses
52. Flash drive filler
53. It was first conquered in 1953
57. '60s White House resident, familiarly
60. Hindi equivalent of Mr.
62. Palindromic mag
63. Something often twisted apart
64. Line after a hard day
66. Dweller along the Danube
67. NY Yankee, e.g.
68. Exodus fare
69. House sitters?
70. Actor Ron and bridge maven Culbertson
71. Wanes

Down

1. Call across vales
2. It makes good scents
3. Borscht veggies
4. Draft pick
5. Crest letters
6. Got out of dodge
7. Bridge authority who starred with Peter in 1962
8. Halfhearted
9. Mao ___-tung
10. Patch up, in a way
11. "Chop-chop!" (abbr.)
12. NY players
13. Act like an ass?
18. Lawless TV character
22. Rodeo female
24. Baby boomers' babies, briefly
26. It has its problems
28. Usher's domain
29. Bridge author Allan
30. Lake not far from Niagara Falls
31. 57-down, e.g.
32. Green card, for short
33. Rappelling need
36. First name of a Fed head

46

Think Twice!

39. Stimulate
40. Cavorted
41. Ancient times
44. Handyman's oeuvre
47. Epinephrine-producing gland
49. Toothy swimmer
50. Many grills
51. Fertilization target
54. Sonia's court colleague
55. "Bad" for "good," e.g.
56. High level transfer
57. 31-down, e.g.
58. Without obligation, like some bids in competition

59. "Smoke Gets In Your Eyes" composer
61. Play ___ role in
64. West from the East
65. "This tape will self-destruct..." org.

Across

1. Fathers, e.g.
4. Beatles' "___ a Place"
10. Hemoglobin-filled transporter (abbr.)
13. H2, for one
14. "Rio Lobo" et al.
15. 1899 warrior
16. Ace
17. Of equal standing
18. Casual greeting
19. Cover letters?
21. Hearts
23. It may hold a spray
25. Manitoba tribesman
27. Alaska's ___ Fjords National Park
28. Canal site
29. "Popeye" surname
30. Poseurs, in surf slang
31. He loved Ilsa
32. Algiers district
34. Grandfather, in "Peter and the Wolf"
36. Free, perhaps
41. Many a big 13-across
43. Free, courtesy of yours truly
44. Whodunit awards
48. Top spot, sometimes
49. Altar procedure
50. DKNY's D
51. Trudge along
52. Shortening used in many recipes
53. Yarborough component
55. Rain check?
56. U2's land, to its natives
57. Z producer
60. Grp. that puts out many schedules
63. "Why not!"
64. A bad gut reaction
65. Pard of 61-down
66. LSAT takers, often
67. Full of mischief
68. One in a shell

Down

1. Eval. unit
2. Place to find a stud?
3. *Leglock, of a sort
4. *Secure position for further advancement
5. First name in "A New Hope"
6. Info at SFO
7. *WWE maneuver
8. Nullify
9. Lat. and Ukr., once
10. *Firm grasp
11. Take off the top?
12. Major crossroads
15. Crammed (up)
20. Keyhole observations
22. *Judo maneuver
23. Hit or miss, e.g.
24. Soprano's song, sometimes
25. Winter quaffs
26. "___ Hope"
30. Like many a bandit in 14-across
33. Good, to Galileo
35. *Storage facility

Not Now!

37. Life line?
38. *It's screwed on at certain gyms
39. "Chicago Hope" extras (abbr.)
40. Finesse starter?
42. Makes a common no trump play, and a hint for the starred clues
44. '50s duds
45. More muddleheaded
46. *Fortress
47. Chips in chips
51. Trojan of fame
54. Years in ancient Rome

55. *Firm mountaineering grip
58. FICA benefit
59. '50s monogram
61. See 65-across
62. Word with White, Red, or Black

Across

1. Pen name?
4. Secretly dupe (abbr.)
7. Put the squeeze on
13. Pistol Pete's sch.
14. Opposite of 20-across
15. Short end of the stick
16. Sniffs out
18. On the table
19. Theo LeSieg was his lesser known pen name
20. Opposite of 14-across
21. Key for some bailouts
22. Contemporary of Sarah and Carmen
23. Do a museum job
25. AOL, e.g.
27. Its max. is 180
29. First Lady Hoover
30. "No turning back now!"
32. Weather
36. Bird feeder filler
37. Foxier?
39. 2001 debut
40. "Who else?"
42. Office tablet
44. ACBL event for duos
45. Wile E. Coyote's supply house
46. Swing, e.g.
47. Off
50. Bridge Circus first?
52. First Lady McKinley
53. Loose lips, so to speak
54. Portmanteau of French words for "velvet" and "hook"
57. Cashes
59. Responded to an xx, perhaps
60. Israeli diet?
61. Embitterment
62. Smattering
63. Underscore, e.g.
64. Stubborn sort
65. Many 27-across takers

Down

1. Sch. campus unit
2. Epiphanic exclamation
3. Darling darlings
4. Blind tenor Andrea
5. Some old Olds
6. They're beside the point (abbr.)
7. Many mani supplies
8. O, to Odysseus
9. O VIPs?
10. Zero
11. Many ex-presidents work for one
12. TVA product
15. U-___ (metro transit)
17. Night sch. staple
20. Libation labeled with a clipper
24. Feed element
25. Minute, informally
26. She starred in "Hamlet 2" as herself
28. Be off
31. "Funny Girl" composer
33. Certain defensive maneuvers, and a hint to four answers in the grid
34. Leonine outburst
35. 13th century Icelandic work

This Puzzle Packs a Wallop

38. Shortener, for short
41. Drifting aimlessly, perhaps
43. Archenemies
47. Papers, for short
48. Public Citizen co-founder
49. Hops kiln
51. Sauce (abbr.)
52. Exasperates
55. Paddler's target, sometimes
56. "Eight ever, nine never" consideration
58. Legal addendum?
59. Fjord's kin

Across

1. Scarab family member
8. Puritanical edict
15. Womb-related
16. Fix the roof, e.g.
17. Duplicates
18. Target of a laser, perhaps
19. Duplicate result (abbr.)
20. Becomes ticked-off
22. Gray matter?
24. Earthshaking experiences
25. They may be ripped, for short
28. Muesli munchable
30. Dr. ___
31. Humble pie, so to speak
32. Sudden influx
35. Buttress
37. Pasta topper
38. JFK served in it
39. Femininst Jong
40. It bites many youngsters
42. Split up
43. Prudence
44. Outdoor outfitter (abbr.)
45. Rocky Mountain tribesman
46. Roxy Music founder
47. "Paradise Lost" poet
49. Start of a JFK quote
52. Material used in ugg boots
54. Locus for connections
56. Popular talk medium
59. Simultaneously
61. Indy scramblers
62. Spun, at the gym
63. Rabbit seasons?
64. In the best of all worlds

Down

1. *Paratrooper's outfit
2. City with a SUNY branch
3. Liz Lemon exclamation
4. Cover when inappropriate, e.g.
5. Lit. genre
6. Tumult
7. Legionnaire Beau
8. Top prize, metaphorically
9. Ones with attachment issues?
10. Netizens, e.g.
11. Alternately
12. Luxurious place?
13. Olympic sprinter ___ Boldon
14. *Piece of boogie boarding gear
21. Hearts, clubs and diamonds, often, and a hint to the six starred clues
23. Fox
25. Degree alternative
26. Game on a lawn
27. *Juicy product?
29. Centuries on end
31. Contacts' contact
32. *Cosmonaut's safety equipment
33. Praline piece, often
34. Jetson often in the doghouse
35. Schmooze (with)
36. Poetic measures
41. More in need of a hosing down
45. Together
47. Member of la familia
48. Congo River Basin mammal

49

Three No Trump?

50. Nut case?
51. Baked noodle pudding
52. Milk (prefix)
53. Network terminal
55. *Onesie, e.g.
56. *Halloween rental, sometimes
57. Nomar's bride
58. ACLU concerns
60. Monogram of a noted
    astronaut

Across

1. Turkish title of old
6. Lord's holding
10. Undercover letters?
13. Former NBA star with a cameo on "Third Rock from the Sun"
14. Out with the buoys
15. Kool Moe Dee's genre
16. Just make
17. Firing chamber
18. First of a Latin trio
19. Place where many threads are removed
21. One of over a dozen popes
22. It's often bid
23. Palindromic bird
24. Game featured in a "Seinfeld" episode
25. Multiple-PC hookup
26. Was worth it, big time
30. Spot for swingers?
32. Spots
33. A slow one is better than a fast one
34. Agent Scully of "The X-Files"
36. Put in a 17-across
37. River nymph of Greek myth
39. 1, often (abbr.)
40. Home of the Tappet Brothers
43. Eliza Doolittle, e.g.
46. Super Bowl IV MVP Dawson
48. Ocean-bottom fish
49. Shaker Society founder Lee
50. "Invisible Cities" author Calvino
52. Whitesnake's "Here ___ Again"
53. Best-selling single of 1956
56. Palindromic female name
57. Goddess who threw a golden apple
58. Greet from afar
59. Sr.'s hurdle
60. Dark time, in brief
61. Laid back
62. Eur. carrier
63. Edamame beans
64. Time unit?

Down

1. Pushed around, as food
2. It pairs with thymine in DNA
3. Biblically belted
4. Drag before a judge
5. Pot contents
6. They're sometimes used to get six-packs (abbr.)
7. Digs
8. Hydroelectricity providers?
9. Zealot's group
10. New Orleans confection
11. "Wall Street" role player
12. Scares
13. Befitting a king
20. Sacred peak in Greek myth (abbr.)
24. No longer down
27. Cable choice
28. Toss
29. Word in many Sue Grafton titles
31. Makes emends?

Blocked Suits

50

35. Sound of relief
36. It's a part of life
37. 2012 Nik Wallenda tightrope walk site
38. Up for grabs
39. Ones tough to keep up with
41. It's on the level
42. Publicist's handout
43. Hard rock bands?
44. Grand slam bid without the ace of trump, e.g.
45. Drum kit parts
47. "Tropic Thunder" actor
51. Lewis Carroll creatures

53. Inspires
54. Pizzazz
55. 1957 movie river

Across

1. CLE listings
5. Name in the Beatles' "Get Back"
9. Keepers of peas on earth?
13. Shellack
14. Sarcastic agreement
15. Still with a chance
16. A director does this
17. LHO part
18. 11,000-foot spouter
19. Part 1 of George S. Kaufman's response, when a partner asked permission to use the men's room
22. Cause of a big splash
23. Recess rebuttal
25. Response, part 2
30. Lexicon's initials
31. "Wait your turn, pal!"
32. Flap and Fuzz of "Beetle Bailey" (abbr.)
33. Famous bridge portmanteau
35. Recesses
38. Orphan girl in "Silas Marner"
42. Information taken from the bidding
43. Contemporary of Boris
47. Blind component
48. In the style of
49. Contract violation
51. Contract negotiator (abbr.)
52. Response, part 3
55. They're low for aces (abbr.)
56. Made ends meet?
57. Response, part 4
63. Red Skelton bumpkin
64. Long, long time
65. Coup target?
66. Atomic reactor part
67. Da ___ (Vietnamese city)
68. Head lines? (abbr.)

Down

1. Play low against a Chinese finesse, e.g.
2. Many a double dummy problem
3. Dummkopf
4. Really rankles
5. Bridge champion Levin
6. Do one's bidding
7. A 33-across first?
8. Sergeant Snorkel's sidekick
9. One of Benito's partners
10. Sidelined, as an ace (abbr.)
11. Patronizes, in a way
12. BART stop
20. They're assigned
21. Get to, as with a psyche
22. BART stop
24. Kvetches' cries
26. Inits. for a film buff
27. PR, so to speak
28. "Got milk?"
29. Extension on some program files
33. Julio, e.g.
34. DJ's spinners
35. Health food berry

36. Bid over pard's double, e.g.
37. Beginning for many measurements
39. Moms' arrangement, often
40. Moor's betrayer
41. Caesarian delivery?
43. Craig's preceder
44. Repugnant exclamation
45. "The ___", popularized by Bergen and Cohen
46. Berlin attention-getter
49. Sons of, in many temple names
50. It might grow on you
53. Last word in doughnuts
54. Nervous giggle
57. One for a knave (abbr.)
58. Pugilistic poet
59. Passing word?
60. Suffix with ball or bass
61. Kvetch
62. Sot's syndrome, for short

ACROSS

1. Minimalist's goal
5. "1812 Overture" player, often
9. Stratego's equivalent of the king
13. Foster or Smith follower
14. As to, in legal memos
15. Big name in pharmaceuticals
17. 4,000 pounds?
19. Theme park acronym
20. Photo finish, of a sort
21. First home, of a sort
22. In yesteryear
25. "No bacon unless you're good!" perhaps?
27. Cold War connection
29. AQI monitor
30. ABA member's title
31. A cappella part
32. Big name in theaters
34. Scout's instruction to a pilot rounding a sharp bend?
40. Place for a boutonniere
41. Asta's lady
43. Olympic sprinter Boldon
46. Parisian possessive
47. Painter who quarreled with Van Gogh
50. Sisters' static?
53. Orestes, to Agamemnon
54. Heebie-jeebies
55. Tart part
57. Chirrup
58. 5-0 and the like, and a hint to 17-, 25-, 34-, and 50-across
62. March site of 1965
63. Parisian possessive
64. Fishing, perhaps
65. Leave in stitches
66. Cause for an upgrade, perhaps
67. It uses RONF

DOWN

1. Plunked down a singleton, e.g.
2. "Foucault's Pendulum" author
3. Wu ___ (Chinese martial art)
4. Blubbers
5. Frisbee forerunner
6. Punctual
7. Many a charity event
8. JFK, once
9. Curve cutters
10. Easy strider
11. Gather over time
12. D&D baddies
16. Bibliographical abbr.
18. Mormon prophet, or the city named for him
21. Let float, as a currency
22. "By Jove!"
23. "A good walk spoiled" according to Twain
24. Inflatable pilot in "Airplane!"
26. Long stretch
28. Veg
32. Part of many rappers' names
33. Tweeted
35. It's sometimes offered to those that go in the tank

1	2	3	4		5	6	7	8		9	10	11	12	
13					14					15				16
17				18						19				
			20						21					
22	23	24		25				26						
27			28					29				30		
31							32				33			
	34			35	36	37						38	39	
			40								41			42
43	44	45		46				47	48	49				
50			51			52						53		
54						55				56				
57						58					59	60	61	
62					63					64				
	65				66					67				

36. Applies the rule of fifteen, e.g.
37. Player who 1-down, in many bridge columns
38. Notes from shy folks?
39. Salt-N-Pepa, e.g.
42. "___ Gallagher finesse" (type of two-way finesse)
43. Some are FDIC-insured
44. Olympic swimmer Dara
45. "Modern Family" star
47. Michael played him in "Wall Street"
48. Jackal-headed deity

49. It broke up in 1991
51. Smarty-pants in the Mystery Machine
52. Caesarean section?
56. Caddies hold them
58. Swinger's selection
59. Simile's linkers
60. Sine qua non
61. Save, for short

SOLUTIONS

C	A	S	A	■	I	V	A	N	■	O	W	E	S	■
O	N	U	S	■	S	I	L	O	■	B	O	L	T	S
Ⓔ	Ⓘ	Ⓖ	Ⓗ	T	B	A	L	L	■	L	O	U	I	E
U	T	A	H	A	N	■	■	T	W	I	D	D	L	E
R	A	R	E	R	■	Ⓔ	Ⓥ	Ⓔ	Ⓡ	G	R	E	E	N
■	■	P	A	P	A	Y	A	■	Y	A	O	■	■	■
S	L	I	P	■	L	I	L	A	■	T	W	O	N	O
P	A	L	■	F	I	N	E	S	S	E	■	Z	I	A
F	O	L	I	O	■	G	R	I	T	■	F	O	L	K
■	■	H	U	G	■	I	C	E	D	I	N	■	■	■
Ⓝ	Ⓘ	Ⓝ	Ⓔ	L	I	V	E	S	■	E	R	E	C	T
A	M	I	A	B	L	E	■	■	H	E	E	H	A	W
T	H	O	R	A	■	Ⓝ	Ⓔ	Ⓥ	Ⓔ	Ⓡ	M	O	R	E
S	I	B	Y	L	■	T	A	S	M	■	A	L	E	E
■	P	E	A	L	■	S	T	O	P	■	N	E	W	T

G	A	R	P	■	E	R	A	T	■	T	I	K	I	S
W	H	O	A	■	C	O	H	O	■	O	B	A	M	A
B	I	O	G	■	H	A	S	P	■	P	E	R	O	N
■	■	K	O	M	Ⓞ	Ⓓ	Ⓞ	Ⓓ	R	A	G	O	N	S
A	S	I	D	E	■	■	O	O	Z	Y	■	■	■	■
S	W	E	A	T	Ⓛ	Ⓞ	Ⓓ	G	E	■	O	B	A	N
H	O	Y	■	R	E	P	O	■	■	T	U	L	S	A
P	O	E	■	I	T	S	Ⓢ	Ⓐ	F	E	■	I	S	P
I	S	A	A	C	■	■	E	L	E	M	■	N	I	L
T	H	R	U	■	H	O	D	G	Ⓔ	Ⓟ	Ⓞ	Ⓓ	G	E
■	■	G	M	E	N	■	■	■	T	R	A	N	S	■
D	U	M	M	Y	R	E	V	E	R	S	A	L	■	■
A	V	I	E	W	■	D	O	R	Y	■	C	L	E	O
H	E	N	N	A	■	G	I	L	A	■	L	E	A	D
L	A	I	T	Y	■	E	D	E	N	■	E	Y	R	E

(3)   You Said It!

A	G	R	A	■	F	E	S	S	■	T	R	A	D	E
D	R	A	W	■	R	A	N	T	■	H	O	B	O	S
Z	E	T	A	■	E	R	O	O	■	E	V	E	N	T
■	W	A	R	R	E	N	B	U	F	F	E	T	T	■
■	■	■	D	E	B	■	S	T	A	B	■	■	■	■
W	I	N	S	B	I	G	■	■	A	I	R	I	L	Y
E	V	A	■	A	D	O	S	E	■	A	M	I	E	■
S	O	M	E	R	S	E	T	M	A	U	G	H	A	M
T	R	E	X	■	■	S	P	U	R	N	■	I	N	E
S	Y	S	T	E	M	■	■	S	M	I	T	T	E	N
■	■	■	N	A	B	C	■	C	O	O	■	■	■	■
■	E	D	G	A	R	A	L	L	A	N	P	O	E	■
S	C	R	A	M	■	M	A	I	N	■	D	A	D	S
P	H	O	T	O	■	B	I	R	D	■	O	H	I	O
R	O	P	E	R	■	I	M	A	Y	■	G	U	T	S

(4)   Without Honor

M	U	T	T	S	■	I	H	O	P	■	N	I	K	E
A	T	E	A	T	■	N	O	V	A	■	O	N	I	T
J	U	N	K	D	R	A	W	E	R	■	R	A	T	A
O	B	O	E	■	O	P	E	N	■	R	U	S	T	S
R	E	R	A	I	S	E	■	■	H	O	S	T	■	■
■	B	U	S	T	O	N	E	S	H	U	M	P	■	■
C	A	R	O	M	■	■	T	O	M	E	■	P	I	A
B	L	O	W	■	T	W	E	R	P	■	W	O	K	S
E	D	U	■	S	O	A	R	■	■	H	I	R	E	S
R	A	G	S	T	O	R	I	C	H	E	S	■	■	■
■	H	E	A	L	■	■	H	A	R	H	A	R	S	■
S	O	N	I	C	■	F	O	U	L	■	B	M	O	C
P	R	E	Z	■	Y	A	R	B	O	R	O	U	G	H
C	E	C	E	■	A	R	A	B	■	U	N	S	E	W
A	S	K	S	■	O	R	L	Y	■	T	E	T	R	A

```
F E B ■ ■ G R A M ■ H O P I S
A S I F ■ A C L U ■ A V A N T
S T R I P M A L L ■ J E T L I
O D D J O B ■ A T M ■ R I A L
■ B I L L ■ ■ N I G H T O W L
A V A ■ L I T ■ ■ M E A ■ ■ ■
C O T T O N G I N ■ S K I P S
E C H O ■ G I N A S ■ E R I E
Y E S W E ■ F I G H T S O N G
■ ■ N T H ■ ■ S A O ■ N E A ■
K E Y C H A I N ■ C A L C ■ ■
N E A R ■ H M O ■ K N U R L S
I N D I E ■ B I L L Y G O A T
S I D E S ■ E R S E ■ E S S O
H E A R T ■ D E U S ■ ■ S T P
```

```
E P A ■ A S T O ■ B R I D G E
G A L ■ S P A R ■ R E T U R N
G R O W S O L D ■ A D A G E S
S E M I N O L E ■ S I L ■ ■ ■
O V A L ■ N O R T H P O L E ■
N E R D S ■ W E B ■ ■ I S U ■
■ ■ W W F ■ D I S S E N T S ■
T A K E A I M ■ R E M A K E S
O L E S T R A ■ D R E S S E R
G O A T H E R D ■ B A T ■ ■ ■
S U N ■ ■ C O O ■ R A M E N ■
■ D E E P S O U T H ■ S O D A
■ ■ N E A ■ B O O K I N G S ■
T O P T E N ■ L O P E A R E D
S W E R V E ■ E L I N ■ O R A
P L A Y E R ■ D E N T ■ E S Q
```

7

A Stone's Throw Away

Puzzle 7 grid:

D	A	H	L		T	H	E	S	E		C	T	R	S
O	N	E	A		H	A	S	O	N		H	E	A	P
Ⓗ	Ⓞ	Ⓟ	U	P	W	I	T	H	T	H	E	A	C	E
A	N	A	G	R	A	M		O	R	D	E	R	E	D
		H	E	R				I	T	S				
	Ⓢ	Ⓚ	Ⓘ	Ⓟ	T	W	O	L	E	V	E	L	S	
B	E	R	T		S	O	R	O	S		L	O	U	D
A	T	E	U	P		N	C	O		H	O	M	M	E
Ⓙ	Ⓤ	Ⓜ	Ⓟ	R	I	G	H	T	T	O	G	A	M	E
A	P	E		I	M	S		S	I	T		N	A	P
		O	N	O				F	W	D				
	T	R	A	C	K	A	N	D	F	I	E	L	D	
R	A	I	S	E		I	O	U		R	E	S	E	T
A	B	O	I	L		D	E	C		E	R	A	S	E
N	U	T	S	Y		E	L	K		S	E	T	I	N

Who's the Boss?

Puzzle 8 grid:

P	I	N	O	T		B	I	T	I	N	G		H	I	H	A	T
A	B	I	T	E		R	A	N	C	H	O		A	N	I	S	E
M	I	C	H	E	L	A	N	G	E	L	O	S	Ⓓ	Ⓐ	Ⓥ	Ⓘ	Ⓓ
	S	E	E	N	A	S				D	E	E	R	E	S		
		P	L	A	Y	I	T	A	G	A	I	N	Ⓢ	Ⓐ	Ⓜ		
F	O	U	L		S	L	A	L	O	M	E	D		G	I	L	T
A	L	T	O	S		D	U	R	O			R	E	N	E	W	
N	E	T		K	I	S	S	M	E	Ⓚ	Ⓐ	Ⓣ	Ⓔ		D	O	O
			A	I	R	Y				D	I	O	R				
	C	A	L	L	A	S	P	A	D	E	A	S	P	A	D	E	
J	E	T	L	I		T	I	M	I	N	G		E	N	U	R	E
A	L	O	A	F		E	N	T	R	E	E		N	U	D	I	E
G	L	I	N	T		M	E	S	S	R	S		S	P	E	C	K

Point Spread

H	O	G		C	H	A	M	P		S	H	O	R	T		L	A	M	B
I	D	O		H	O	N	O	R		T	U	X	E	S		E	V	E	R
F	I	F	T	E	E	N	M	I	N	U	T	E	S	O	F	F	A	M	E
I	S	A	A	C		I	M	N	O		U	N	O		A	T	S	E	A
S	T	R	O	K	E		I	C	U	S			L	A	C		T	S	K
			S	I	X	T	E	E	N	C	A	N	D	L	E	S			
E	T	C		N	T	H		S	O	L	E		G	F	O	R	C	E	
P	R	O	M	O		E	L	O		R	C	A	S		A	D	I	O	S
S	E	V	E	N	T	E	E	N	Y	E	A	R	C	I	C	A	D	A	S
O	V	E	R		E	N	A	C	T		P	L	A	N	T		E	S	A
M	I	R	E		A	D	D	E	D		P	Y	R	E	S		S	T	Y

10

Computer Bridge

M	E	A	N		P	S	I		I	S	T	O
I	N	N	S		E	L	S		S	T	O	P
S	H	I	F	T	T	O	A	T	R	U	M	P
D	A	S		A	R	A	B	I	A			
E	N	T	E	R	A	N	E	V	E	N	T	
E	C	O	L			L	O	L	I	T	A	
D	E	N	I	A	L	S		I	C	O	N	
		A	N	Y	H	O	O		A	P	T	
	C	O	N	T	R	O	L	B	I	D	S	
S	I	C		H	E	R	E	O	N			
O	R	E	O		T	O	E	C	A	P	S	
S	C	A	L	P	S			A	N	A	L	
	E	N	D	U	P	D	O	W	N	O	N	E
		B	R	A	I	S	E		M	A	E	
I	N	S	E	R	T	T	H	E	J	A	C	K
N	A	P	A		E	T	E		A	L	E	E
S	P	A	N		S	O	A		R	Y	A	N

P	T	A	S			R	U	B	S		T	B	S	P
A	I	D	A		S	A	N	A	A		O	L	E	O
R	A	V	I		K	N	O	C	K	K	N	O	C	K
		A	D	M	I	T		K	E	A		C	L	E
P	I	N	O	T	N	O	I	R		Y	O	K	U	M
R	I	C	K	I			T	O	G		R	E	D	O
S	I	E		D	A	W	S	O	N		E	D	E	N
		M	A	N	O	A	M	A	N	O				
C	H	I	A		T	O	S	S	T	O		W	A	R
R	A	N	G		I	D	I		O	R	A	T	E	
I	N	U	I	T		S	N	O	T	N	O	S	E	D
P	D	T		W	A	H		D	I	S	C	O		
P	H	E	N	O	M	E	N	O	N		K	N	I	T
L	O	R	E		A	D	O	R	E		O	T	O	S
E	G	O	S		S	S	R	S		N	O	N	O	

P	O	T		S	L	A	M		A	B	S	O	R	B
U	G	H		M	I	L	A		B	A	I	L	E	Y
P	L	U	G	U	G	L	Y		U	R	G	E	N	T
S	E	M	I		H	A	I	G		T	N	O	T	E
	B	L	O	T		E	S	A	S					
C	L	E	A	R		C	O	R	K	B	O	A	R	D
A	O	L		B	A	H	A	M	A		F	L	E	E
M	U	I	R		L	E	T	A	T		F	L	E	A
P	I	N	E		I	R	E	N	E	S		Y	S	L
S	E	A	L	S	K	I	N	S		L	A	S	E	S
		A	C	E	S		N	O	A	H				
S	A	T	Y	R		H	U	G	O		R	E	F	I
P	R	O	B	E	D		S	T	O	P	P	E	R	S
A	E	R	I	A	L		D	O	N	T		D	E	I
M	A	N	D	M	S		A	S	E	A		Y	E	S

S	E	T	H		B	E	G	A	T		S	T	A	G
I	R	O	C		O	M	A	H	A		L	U	C	Y
(K)	(E)	(E)	(P)	Y	O	U	R	S	H	I	R	T	O	N
H	I	S	S	A	T			I	N	S	U	L	T	
			N	E	E		E	T	A					
(I)	(T)	T	A	K	E	S	A	V	I	L	L	A	G	E
P	A	I	R	S		T	W	O		L	I	N	E	R
A	L	M	A		N	O	O	K	S		E	D	N	A
(S)	(I)	(M)	(P)	(L)	(E)	P	L	E	A	S	U	R	E	S
S	A	Y		O	W	S		D	N	A		E	S	E
		O	K	S			D	U	H					
(S)	(T)	(U)	(P)	(I)	(D)	P	E	T	T	R	I	C	K	S
W	I	R	E		E	A	T	E	R		C	H	A	P
A	K	I	N		S	U	T	R	A		K	I	T	E
K	I	S	S		K	L	U	M	P		S	A	Y	C

14

Hand of a Lifetime

A	L	L	A		B	A	W	L		B	M	A	J
P	A	A	R		O	L	E	O		S	L	I	C	E
L	U	R	K		Z	E	A	L		C	A	C	H	E
O	R	E		R	O	C	K	C	R	U	S	H	E	R
M	E	D	E	A		A	O	R	T	A		
B	L	O	C	K	B	U	S	T	E	R		E	T	S
	L	E	A	N	T		Y	A	L	I	E
A	Q	U	A		M	O	O	S	E		L	S	A	T
K	U	N	T	A		P	I	V	O	T
C	O	D		M	O	N	S	T	E	R	H	A	N	D
	E	L	O	R	O		Y	O	W	I	E
S	I	R	H	U	G	O	D	R	A	X		H	P	S
A	K	B	A	R		D	O	U	R		L	I	P	O
W	E	I	S	S		L	O	N	G		I	L	E	T
N	A	D	A		E	R	G	O		Z	E	R	O

A Turn of Phrase 1

B	O	X	E	S		R	I	P	E		O	P	E	N
O	P	R	A	H		E	R	O	S		N	O	L	A
L	E	A	P	I	N	G	M	I	C	H	A	E	L	S
T	R	Y		V	E	G	A	N		O	U	T	A	T
		M	E	S	A		T	A	R	T
I	N	V	E	R	T	E	D	M	I	N	O	R	S
Z	O	O	M	S		E	A	R	S		E	A	T
O	T	T	O		T	A	W	N	Y		T	I	N	O
D	I	E		U	S	M	A		T	O	K	Y	O
	T	R	U	M	P	P	R	O	M	O	T	I	O	N
		L	A	S	E		N	I	R	O
P	S	A	L	M		R	U	S	S	O		F	E	E
E	L	I	M	I	N	A	T	I	O	N	P	L	A	Y
T	A	D	A		A	G	E	D		T	E	A	S	E
A	M	E	N		P	E	P	E		O	P	T	E	D

Top Players

L	I	K	E	■	O	P	E	N	E	R	■	A	N	K	H
T	O	R	I	■	A	R	M	A	D	A	■	V	E	N	A
D	W	I	G	H	T	E	I	S	E	N	H	O	W	E	R
S	A	S	H	A	■	P	L	A	N	■	O	C	T	E	T
■	■	T	V	A	■	■	■	N	R	A	■	■	■	■	■
■	M	O	H	A	N	D	A	S	G	A	N	D	H	I	■
C	O	N	S	■	D	R	A	P	E	D	■	O	U	T	S
A	B	E	■	E	G	O	M	A	N	I	A	■	M	A	A
W	I	N	S	T	O	N	C	H	U	R	C	H	I	L	L
S	L	O	T	H	■	E	O	N	S	■	T	O	D	O	S
■	■	E	A	U	■	■	■	S	I	B	■	■	■	■	■
■	D	E	N	G	X	I	A	O	P	I	N	G	■	■	■
C	O	U	P	■	L	E	N	T	T	O	■	O	A	R	S
A	B	E	L	■	I	N	T	O	T	O	■	B	M	O	C
R	I	S	E	■	S	A	L	M	O	N	■	S	E	T	H

His & Hers

R	U	F	F	■	P	I	P	E	D	■	A	L	O	T
E	S	A	I	■	A	M	O	R	E	■	R	O	P	E
F	O	R	D	A	S	P	I	R	E	■	E	V	E	N
■	■	E	L	S	E	■	■	O	N	E	N	D	■	■
P	A	T	■	F	A	I	N	T	P	R	A	I	S	E
S	C	H	W	A	S	■	A	R	E	S	■	S	E	R
I	S	E	E	■	S	P	A	D	E	■	B	A	S	■
■	D	E	A	T	H	S	P	I	R	A	L	■	■	■
A	M	A	■	S	A	L	T	S	■	W	I	K	I	■
D	A	R	■	K	N	E	E	■	D	O	W	N	E	R
A	N	K	L	E	S	P	R	A	I	N	■	D	Y	E
P	O	S	E	D	■	■	M	A	K	E	■	■	■	■
T	W	I	G	■	M	I	X	E	D	P	A	I	R	S
T	A	D	A	■	O	V	I	N	E	■	S	P	A	T
O	R	E	L	■	D	E	I	S	M	■	T	O	N	Y

Twice as Nice

```
W E I R S ■ L O U T S ■ A T T
C A M E L ■ E S S I E ■ C I O
S U P P O R T H O S E ■ T P K
■ R A I S E ■ ■ R I T E
D M C ■ N E G A T I V E I O N
J A Y L E N O ■ H O O D I E S
S I T A ■ ■ S E T I N ■
■ D O U B L E H E A D E R S
■ G A I L Y ■ ■ S E A T
A N T H I L L ■ P A S S I V E
P E N A L T Y K I C K ■ N E E
P L O T ■ ■ E N L A I
A L T ■ T A K E O U T F O O D
L I E ■ S L E P T ■ E F I L E
L E S ■ A B Y S S ■ D Y L A N
```

19

Switching Things Up

```
M A J O R ■ V I L A ■ B R A E
A M E B A ■ A K I N ■ J A C K
D I D I T ■ L E V I ■ O T O E
A G I ■ A P U ■ E M E R A L D
M A K A B L E ■ W A L K ■
■ N A L A ■ D I L L ■ B R A
F B I M E N ■ A R R ■ S L A M
L U G E ■ T O M E I ■ W I K I
A C H S ■ N U N ■ G A I N E D
T K T ■ G U T S ■ H I N D
■ M O R T ■ S T R E A K Y
F R A I D S O ■ A S K ■ L O O
L I O N ■ E S P N ■ I N L A W
I S N O ■ R E A D ■ S H E L L
P E E R ■ Y A W S ■ S L Y A S
```

B	L	A	H		P	A	R	D		C	H	I	C
R	A	M	A		A	M	E	R		L	E	C	H
A	L	A	N		P	I	C	O		A	L	A	I
S	A	N	D	B	A	G		W	E	I	G	H	T
I	W	A	S	A	Y	O	U	N	G	M	A	N	
		D	N	A		S	S	A					
T	A	H	O	E		O	H	I	D	U	N	N	O
S	L	O	W		W	H	E	N		P	L	A	Y
O	P	E	N	S	E	A	S		I	T	E	M	S
			O	E	R		A	S	H				
	T	H	I	S	D	E	A	L	B	E	G	A	N
T	H	E	M	O	B		P	E	N	A	L	T	Y
H	E	A	P		G	E	I	R		N	O	A	M
E	T	R	E		O	A	S	T		T	O	R	E
N	A	T	L		N	T	H	S		E	M	I	T

H	C	P		E	V	I	N	C	E		F	T	L	B
A	A	A		S	A	M	I	A	M		E	R	I	E
S	T	R	I	P	T	E	A	S	E		A	U	R	A
I	C	E	R			A	S	T	R		T	M	A	N
T	H	R	O	W	I	N		R	I	P	U	P		
			C	O	N	T	R	O	L	F	R	E	A	K
U	N	S		O	K	I	E			C	E	D	A	R
C	A	P	N		S	T	A	G	S		S	I	R	I
S	T	O	O	D			D	R	I	P		N	E	S
B	O	T	T	O	M	F	E	E	D	E	R			
		C	A	C	A	O		A	E	R	O	B	A	T
S	T	A	C		D	R	A	T			O	L	L	A
K	A	R	L		D	O	U	B	L	E	T	A	L	K
U	R	D	U		E	N	N	U	I	S		S	E	E
A	P	S	E		R	E	T	Y	P	E		T	Y	S

22

Wake-up Call

B	A	B	O	O		S	H	U	I		R	I	S	D
A	L	O	O	P		Q	U	I	D		E	S	A	U
S	I	X	F	I	G	U	R	E	I	N	C	O	M	E
S	E	C		U	N	I	T			Y	E	L	P	
I	N	A		M	U	D		H	U	S	S	A	R	S
S	T	R	A	W	S		F	I	V	E	S	T	A	R
T	O	S	E	A		M	A	L	E			E	S	S
			D	R	E	A	M	L	A	N	D			
A	L	A			A	X	E	S		I	N	E	R	T
C	O	M	E	O	V	E	R		S	T	A	M	O	S
S	W	E	L	L	E	D		P	E	P		O	T	O
	B	R	E	D			H	E	M	I		T	U	N
A	L	I	V	E	A	N	D	K	I	C	K	I	N	G
C	O	K	E		V	E	T	O		K	I	N	D	A
E	W	A	N		G	A	V	E		S	A	G	A	S

23

It's a Feature!

G	R	I	F	T		C	E	N	T		S	D	A	K
L	I	M	O	S		O	R	S	O		L	O	D	E
A	P	P	L	E	J	U	I	C	E		A	G	H	A
D	E	S	K		U	P	C		A	L	T	O	N	
			H	A	D		A	I	R	F	O	R	C	E
E	F	F	E	N	D	I		N	O	R	M	A		
T	I	A	R	A		R	U	S	T			I	A	M
A	G	H	O	S	T	O	F	A	C	H	A	N	C	E
S	S	R			I	N	O	N		A	C	E	T	O
	E	N	O	K	I		E	A	T	C	R	O	W	
A	N	N	E	R	I	C	E		C	S	I			
R	E	H	A	B		N	E	A		D	R	A	B	
E	W	E	R		O	U	T	S	I	D	E	A	C	E
N	E	I	L		P	R	E	P		A	N	G	I	E
A	R	T	Y		T	U	R	N		S	T	U	D	S

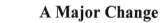

B	U	S	T		O	C	T	A	D			S	P	A
A	N	K	H		S	H	O	R	T		Q	T	I	P
N	E	A	R	T	H	I	N	G	S		U	R	A	L
		O	V	A	R	Y			L	E	O	N	A	
S	C	H	W	A		P	A	R	T	H	E	N	O	N
B	R	A	N	D	I		O	R	A	N	G	S		
A	E	R	I		C	A	C	T	U	S				
	D	I	N	N	E	R	T	H	E	A	T	E	R	
		A	T	O	A	S	T			A	S	I	S	
	C	O	W	P	E	A			O	B	L	A	D	I
I	N	T	H	E	A	R	E	A		O	K	I	E	S
V	O	T	E	S		V	O	I	D	S				
A	T	A	T		H	E	A	R	T	S	H	I	F	T
N	E	W	S		R	E	N	T	S		O	R	G	Y
A	S	A		E	S	S	A	Y		P	A	S	S	

C	U	P			P	R	U	D	E			G	A	B
O	N	A		D	E	E	P	E	N	S		O	L	E
H	E	Y	D	I	D	D	L	E	D	I	D	D	L	E
E	S	P	Y	S		T	A	J		L	E	A	D	S
N	C	A	A		S	I	N	A	I		A	R	A	T
	O	L	D	F	U	D	D	Y	D	U	D	D	Y	
		E	V	E		S	A	G						
A	T	E	A	T						L	E	A	P	T
Y	A	D	D	A	Y	A	D	D	A	Y	A	D	D	A
E	R	G	O		O	V	E	R	T		T	V	A	D
S	E	E	N		N	O	P	U	N		S	I	S	S
	S	I	X	D	I	A	M	O	N	D	S			
I	L	O	S	T		D	R	S		A	I	O	L	I
L	A	U	E	R		E	T	E		E	R	R	O	R
L	O	T	S	A		D	S	T		S	T	Y	L	E

Easley Does It

T	U	G	A	T		P	R	O	A	M		S	A	C
E	V	I	T	E		O	O	M	P	A		C	R	O
Ⓝ	E	R	V	E	Ⓣ	I	S	S	U	E		O	S	U
S	A	D		T	O	N	I				I	N	O	N
		Ⓝ	E	W	Ⓣ	E	S	T	A	M	E	N	T	
T	A	V	E	R	N	S		O	H	N	O			
G	N	A	W	S			4	R	U	N	N	E	R	S
I	T	I	S		A	C	N	E	D		F	L	E	A
F	E	L	L	F	L	A	T		R	I	S	E	N	
		E	T	A	L		E	M	E	R	A	L	D	
Ⓝ	O	M	A	D	I	C	Ⓣ	R	I	B	E			
A	M	O	K			U	R	S	A		J	U	S	
G	I	L		Ⓝ	O	R	D	I	C	Ⓣ	R	A	C	K
A	T	L		O	N	I	O	N		E	A	G	L	E
T	S	O		R	E	O	R	G		S	T	R	A	W

P	B	J		E	X	P	E	L		E	X	P	O	S
O	R	O		A	I	S	L	E		D	R	U	R	Y
M	I	N	E	R	S	U	I	T		S	A	R	A	N
S	O	B	E	L			A	S	S		Y	A	L	E
	O	R	A	T	E		A	H	A	S				
P	A	N		P	H	A	N	T	O	M	P	E	A	R
L	B	J		S	I	T	E		W	I	E	N	I	E
U	H	O	H		R	S	V	P	D		X	T	R	A
M	O	V	E	I	T		E	L	O	I		H	E	P
B	R	I	D	G	E	C	R	E	W	S		U	S	S
	G	A	E	A		A	N	A	I	S				
C	R	U	E		N	R	A		P	R	I	M	E	
L	I	G	H	T		L	I	M	I	T	R	A	Y	S
I	G	L	O	O		O	D	I	S	T		S	T	P
P	A	I	G	E		T	A	B	O	O		T	H	Y

P	D	F	S		B	U	N	K	S		B	A	I	L
R	E	U	P		E	M	I	L	E		U	R	S	A
O	L	L	A		S	A	N	A	(A)		(C)(E)	N	T	
V	E	L	C	R	O		A	L	O	H	A	O	E	
	S	E	E	T	O	I	T		N	A	S	T		
R	I	C	(K)(I)		(N)(G)	U	Y	E	N					
U	S	A		C	A	N		O	N	A	B	E	T	
S	P	L	I	T	O	N	E	S	H	O	N	O	R	S
H	Y	E	N	A	S		O	H	O		T	I	A	
	C	L	I	(Q)(U)(E)		(E)(N)	T	E	R					
	S	H	U	I		U	S	S	T	E	E	L		
A	L	A	B	A	M	A		R	O	G	E	T	S	
B	A	(J)(A)		(C)(K)	O	N	E		A	D	O	T		
I	M	I	T		A	E	R	I	E		T	U	N	A
E	S	S	E		T	R	E	A	D		E	P	I	C

S	P	A	R	■	H	E	L	I	X	■	J	A	M	S
A	L	L	A	■	A	S	A	D	A	■	U	V	E	A
C	U	L	B	E	R	T	S	O	N	■	M	I	N	I
■	M	Y	B	A	D	■	E	T	A	■	P	A	S	S
■	■	M	I	S	S	M	■	O	D	O	R	■	■	
A	M	C	■	T	H	E	F	O	U	R	A	C	E	S
B	A	B	U	■	I	M	O	■	■	G	I	L	D	A
A	T	E	N	■	P	E	C	O	S	■	S	O	I	R
C	R	A	B	S	■	■	A	X	E	■	E	T	T	A
K	I	L	L	I	N	G	L	E	A	D	■	H	S	N
■	■	O	B	O	E	■	S	W	I	P	E	■	■	
I	M	A	C	■	O	R	S	■	O	D	I	S	T	■
R	O	C	K	■	G	U	M	W	R	A	P	P	E	R
O	T	O	E	■	I	N	O	I	L	■	P	I	S	H
C	O	L	D	■	E	D	G	E	D	■	I	N	T	O

S	T	A	G	S	■	S	T	D	■	O	S	C	A	R
W	O	R	R	Y	■	Q	U	O	■	P	A	R	L	E
I	B	E	A	M	■	U	R	U	■	T	C	E	L	L
N	O	O	N	■	S	E	R	B	S	■	R	A	M	A
G	O	L	D	■	L	E	E	L	A	■	I	S	A	Y
S	T	E	S	■	A	Z	T	E	C	■	F	E	N	S
■	■	L	A	N	E	■	S	H	U	I	■	■		
A	T	L	A	S	T	■	■	A	S	C	O	T	S	
C	H	A	M	P	■	O	C	T	■	E	E	N	I	E
T	O	M	■	■	I	M	H	I	P	■	R	A	T	
■	■	B	R	I	D	G	E	T	A	B	L	E	■	
■	P	A	I	N	T	■	■	T	R	I	C	K	■	
B	A	S	E	B	A	L	L	D	I	A	M	O	N	D
I	N	T	L	■	G	E	T	I	N	■	B	R	E	R
D	E	E	S	■	S	I	D	E	A	■	O	D	E	S

H	I	D		G	O	L	E	M		P	E	K	E	S
A	N	O		A	L	A	M	O		H	O	I	S	T
H	O	W	D	O	E	S	I	T	F	E	E	L	T	O
A	N	N	O			L	I	O	N		L	A	P	
		G	I	G	I		F	R	O	M	E			
P	L	A	Y	W	I	T	H		M	A	D	A	M	
S	I	L		O	N	S	A	L	E		I	T	S	Y
H	E	L	E	N	S	O	B	E	L	S	M	I	T	H
A	T	T	N		U	N	L	A	D	E		M	I	A
W	O	O	E	D			A	N	E	X	P	E	R	T
	O	R	E	A	D		S	R	T	A				
H	I	S		X	R	A	Y			R	A	V	I	
I	D	O	N	T	K	N	O	W	A	S	K	H	I	M
S	N	O	R	E		T	W	I	N	E		M	A	P
S	O	N	A	R		E	L	I	T	E		E	L	S

R	A	C	E		T	I	F	F		B	I	D	S	
I	M	A	N		A	D	O	T		G	L	O	A	T
T	O	P	D	O	L	L	A	R		R	U	N	B	Y
U	N	L	U	C	K	Y	L	O	U	I	E			
A	R	E	S	T			O	A	F		G	N	U	
L	A	T	E		G	R	A	P	E	F	R	U	I	T
		E	T	A	L			I	H	A	T	E		
	M	I	N	N	I	E	B	O	T	T	O	M	S	
V	A	N	E	D		E	V	A	H					
C	Y	T	H	E	C	Y	N	I	C		S	L	U	G
R	O	O		A	P	E			P	A	I	N	E	
	F	R	A	N	K	S	T	E	W	A	R	T		
A	R	G	U	E		N	O	W	O	R	R	I	E	S
B	O	A	R	D		E	L	I	S		E	S	A	I
E	D	G	Y		D	A	M	S		D	E	L	T	

33

A Turn of Phrase 2

S	N	O	O	P	■	A	C	E	S	■	R	S	V	P
T	O	R	U	S	■	N	A	T	E	■	E	P	I	C
R	E	C	T	I	F	Y	T	H	E	C	O	U	N	T
S	L	A	B	■	E	H	S	■	■	A	P	R	E	S
■	■	■	U	N	T	O	■	D	A	R	E	■	■	■
■	Z	E	R	O	T	O	L	E	R	A	N	C	E	■
H	O	L	S	T	■	■	O	M	I	T	■	O	X	O
I	N	I	T	■	S	T	R	I	P	■	I	S	T	O
M	E	H	■	A	T	O	N	■	■	O	N	T	O	P
■	D	U	M	M	Y	R	E	V	E	R	S	A	L	■
■	■	I	B	E	T	■	■	I	A	G	O	■	■	■
A	I	O	L	I	■	■	S	A	C	■	M	P	A	A
S	P	L	I	T	T	I	N	G	H	O	N	O	R	S
H	O	L	E	■	O	M	A	R	■	P	I	T	C	H
E	S	A	U	■	Y	O	G	A	■	S	A	S	S	Y

Repeat Business

S	P	A	R	K	■	F	L	A	K	■	A	F	A	R
O	L	D	I	E	■	L	A	R	A	■	R	I	C	E
D	U	M	M	Y	D	U	M	M	Y	■	M	R	E	D
A	M	I	■	C	O	X	E	S	■	L	A	S	S	O
S	E	T	■	A	P	E	■	D	A	U	N	T	■	■
■	■	■	B	R	I	D	G	E	B	R	I	D	G	E
A	D	D	E	D	■	■	R	A	C	K	■	O	R	R
L	E	A	D	■	O	P	A	L	S	■	S	W	A	G
E	E	L	■	B	R	A	S	■	■	R	O	N	D	O
S	P	A	D	E	S	S	P	A	D	E	S	■	■	■
■	■	I	N	G	O	T	■	T	E	A	■	T	W	A
A	T	L	A	S	■	L	A	B	E	L	■	E	R	N
T	E	A	L	■	M	I	X	E	D	M	I	X	E	D
M	A	M	A	■	U	F	O	S	■	E	R	A	S	E
S	T	A	B	■	D	E	N	T	■	N	E	S	T	S

Judgment Call

P	A	L	M	■	■	N	T	H	■	■	E	S	T	O	S
A	M	I	E	■	G	O	R	E	■	A	C	O	R	N	S
R	A	P	T	■	A	C	O	L	■	T	H	R	E	A	T
■	J	O	H	N	P	A	U	L	S	T	E	V	E	N	S
■	O	P	E	N	■	■	L	I	L	I					
S	A	N	D	R	A	D	A	Y	O	C	O	N	N	O	R
L	E	E	■	T	O	J	O	■	■	N	O	O	N	E	
A	R	A	B	S	■	A	R	T	S	■	■	T	U	N	
W	I	L	L	I	A	M	R	E	H	N	Q	U	I	S	T
■	A	T	M	E	■	R	O	U	T						
T	H	E	S	U	P	R	E	M	E	C	O	U	R	T	
A	O	R	T	A	L	■	A	R	E	A	■	R	I	A	L
T	W	E	E	T	Y	■	S	E	N	T	■	N	A	N	A
S	L	I	D	E	■	T	S	O	■	■	S	A	K	S	

Many, in Marseilles?

S	L	I	N	G	■	S	E	G	O	■	S	R	S
M	Y	B	A	D	■	S	A	R	A	N	■	C	E	O
T	R	U	M	P	T	O	W	E	R	S	■	H	A	R
P	I	P	E	■	A	L	I	■	D	I	M	W	I	T
C	R	O	C	O	D	I	L	E	T	E	A	R	S	
■	O	N	U	S	■	E	N	E	R					
I	N	F	E	R	■	S	E	M	I	■	C	H	I	P
L	E	E	■	B	A	T	H	M	A	T	■	O	P	T
L	O	N	I	■	L	I	S	A	■	A	F	R	O	S
■	M	A	C	E	■	I	R	I	S					
V	I	E	N	N	A	S	A	U	S	A	G	E	S	
N	O	S	O	A	P	■	S	N	L	■	T	R	O	Y
E	N	S	■	C	O	U	P	D	E	G	R	A	C	E
C	I	A	■	I	N	T	O	O	■	R	E	C	A	P
K	A	Y	■	N	E	A	T	■	R	E	E	L	S	

Leaders of the Pack

```
P S I   H O N E       S L A Y
A P R   O R A N G   N Y E T S
R I O   C E N T I   I N A L L
A N N(A)(K)O U R N I K O V A
S D A K       S T I P E N D
O L G(A)(K)O R B U T   S I T H
L Y E   N I N A   P E N A L
    M I L(A)(K)U N I S
A B B O T   E L A N   S S S
F E E T   E A R T H(A)(K)I T T
R A M J E T S     I T O O
  T O U C H I N G H O N O R S
C L A S H   D A L E S   U M S
L E N T O   E B E R T   T I E
E S S E     C E D E   S N L
```

38

Bridge on the Mind 2

```
S M U R F   L O R I   O T T O
L O S E R   I C E T   L E A P
A T S E A   N A S H   A S P S
W O R K I N G S T I F F S
    L O U   A N Y   E L F
  C O N T R A C T K I L L E R
M A L A Y   A E S   I L S A
E N D O   C A N D O   E A S T
C O M M   A L E   A U T O S
C L A I M S A D J U S T E R
A A S   O H S   O A K
  T R I C K Q U E S T I O N
O R E O   R A E S   O O M P A
D I R T   O N I T   U M P E D
D A S H   P S I S   T E S L A
```

A	G	R	A		P	A	U	L	I		B	R	U	T
L	O	E	W		O	U	T	E	D		O	E	N	O
L	A	V	A		P	E	N	A	L		A	V	I	S
	H	E	R	C	U	L	E	P	O	I	R	O	T	
C	E	R	E	A	L			V	O	D	K	A	S	
H	A	S		T	I	G	H	T	E	N		E	R	A
I	D	E	A		S	H	O	U	T		I	D	D	O
			J	A	M	E	S	B	O	N	D			
D	U	C	A	T		E	T	A		U	N	P	E	G
A	R	A	R	A	T			A	T	O	A	S	T	
M	I	R		R	A	S	C	A	L	S		N	C	O
	P	H	I	L	E	A	S	F	O	G	G			
S	H	O	O		C	E	S	A	R		R	A	F	T
T	O	O	L		U	T	I	L	E		A	E	O	N
L	I	L	Y		M	O	O	E	D		B	A	R	T

40 Under Pressure

R	A	S	P	E	D		P	I	U		B	I	B	B
E	X	H	A	L	E		I	N	S		O	N	E	A
D	E	I	C	E	S		◆	C	O	U	N	T	E	R
◆	T	R	I	C	K	S		O	P	S		H	R	E
	O	E	N			E	D	M	E	E	S	E		
		O	D	D	E	V	E	N	D	I	S	◆	S	
O	O	F		T	O	D	D	S			L	O	I	S
A	R	O	U	S	E			S	I	O	U	A	N	
T	Z	U	S			C	O	W	E	D		P	C	S
H	O	L	D	A	L	L	T	H	E	◆	S			
	M	A	F	I	O	S	I			L	I	S		
T	A	O		O	Z	S		M	E	N	A	C	E	◆
S	Q	U	E	E	Z	E	◆		R	A	M	A	P	O
A	U	T	O		I	I	I		I	S	O	N	T	O
R	A	H	S		E	N	O		K	A	N	T	A	R

41 Just Short

G	E	R	B	E	R		E	S	T	A		C	S	A
O	L	E	O	L	E		D	R	O	P		R	U	N
N	O	S	O	A	P		G	A	M	B	L	I	N	G
		K	I	O	W	A	S		I	S	L	S		
S	P	L	I	N	T	E	R		B	B	Q	P	I	T
O	H	O		E	S	A		P	R	O	U	S	T	
S	A	V	E		K	A	R	A	T	E				
	T	E	X	A	S	T	R	A	N	S	F	E	R	
	A	L	L	W	E	T			Y	S	E	R		
	B	O	L	E	R	O		T	C	I		S	A	O
N	A	N	T	E	S		F	L	A	N	N	E	R	Y
E	R	S	E		A	I	E	L	L	O				
V	O	I	D	W	O	O	D		L	E	T	S	G	O
E	N	D		P	O	K	E		T	A	I	L	E	D
R	Y	E		M	O	S	S		O	F	F	O	N	E

42 Well, Duh!

A	R	U	B	A	■	P	F	F	T	■	A	C	B	L
C	O	N	A	N	■	H	A	I	R	■	T	H	A	I
R	A	B	B	I	S	R	U	L	E	■	T	I	R	E
E	R	I	K	■	I	A	N	■	S	O	A	P	E	D
■	D	A	W	G	S	■	A	C	D	C	■			
A	B	S	■	W	H	E	N	T	H	E	K	I	N	G
S	L	U	F	F	■	U	R	I	■	I	N	A	N	
S	O	I	R	■	H	A	D	A	C	■	N	E	N	A
A	T	T	A	■	I	I	I	■	A	G	E	N	T	
I	S	S	I	N	G	L	E	T	O	N	■	D	A	S
■	D	O	H	S	■	R	A	S	T	A	■			
L	L	O	Y	D	S	■	S	O	S	■	W	H	A	P
S	Y	N	C	■	P	L	A	Y	T	H	E	A	C	E
A	R	E	A	■	O	G	R	E	■	R	E	N	A	L
T	E	S	T	■	T	S	A	R	■	E	D	D	I	E

43 Use the Force

S	A	C	K	■	F	L	A	T	■	S	H	E	A
P	L	A	N	A	■	E	A	C	H	■	H	E	L	M
E	L	S	O	L	■	M	I	T	E	■	A	R	T	I
C	A	(T)	(W)	(O)	M	A	N	■	A	(T)	(W)	(O)	O	D
■	(O)	(N)	(E)	I	L	■	A	T	(O)	(N)	(E)	R	S
A	L	F	■	M	E	A	N	E	R	■	S	O	T
S	O	F	T	I	E	■	C	D	R	O	M	■
H	A	S	A	T	■	2	/	1	■	I	C	E	U	P
■	R	S	V	P	D	■	K	D	L	A	N	G
A	L	I	■	O	R	A	C	L	E	■	R	E	A
P	O	S	T	D	O	C	■	I	N	G	O	T	■
P	S	E	U	D	O	■	F	O	O	(T)	(W)	(O)	R	K
L	E	E	R	■	M	O	A	N	■	(O)	(N)	(E)	A	L
E	R	I	N	■	E	L	L	E	■	S	U	A	V	E
S	S	T	S	■	D	E	A	L	■	P	R	I	E

```
B O Y L E   ■ R E G ■ A L A N
O N E I L   ■ O E N O ■ N A T O
D E A L T   ■ H D T V ■ C L E O
■ H A R D W A R E C H A I N ■
■ ■ B A I O ■ ■ R O O S T S ■
T E N N I S W I N N E R ■ ■ ■
A R L E N ■ ■ N E O N ■ G O T
T I E R ■ R A D A R ■ C A P O
A C R ■ R A N I ■ O O Z E D ■
■ B A N D A G E B R A N D ■ ■
O R T E G A ■ O L L A ■ ■ ■
V E N T U R A O F F I L M ■
A L O T ■ I S L E ■ G S U I T
T A T E ■ S T I R ■ E E N S Y
E Y E R ■ K I N ■ S A G O S
```

Hand to Hand Combat

```
  E N T R Y
  M A R I O ■ B A S I C ■ E M M E
  I C I N G ■ A L I T O ■ N O O N
  L H A S A ■ R O R E M ■ R U N T
  S O L O P A R T S ■ B O I L E R
  ■ ■ O R I ■ P A U C I T Y
  T R A N S P O R T A T I O N
  R A I S E ■ A H I ■
  E M M A ■ H O N O R ■ F A D E
  ■ ■ A L G ■ S O L I D
  ■ O U T S I D E E N T R I E S
E M A N U E L ■ L E O
N A T T E R ■ C O D E N A M E S
T R I O ■ A B O V E ■ E L E N A
R I E L ■ P O L E S ■ A L A S T
Y A R D ■ H A D N T ■ G E N O A
                    E N T R Y
```

Y	A	B	B	A		J	O	L	T		J	A	M	B
O	R	E	A	D		E	M	U	S		U	S	E	R
D	O	E	S	A	X	T	A	K	E		R	A	T	A
E	M	T	S		E	T	R	E		G	Y	P	S	Y
L	A	S	A	G	N	E		W	E	A	R			
	L	E	A	D	S	A	X	L	I	F	E			
K	A	R	E	N		E	R	A		G	A	R	B	
I	M	O		X	W	H	A	M	M	Y		L	I	E
D	E	P	O		H	A	T		O	A	K	E	N	
	X	E	D	G	E	D	S	W	O	R	D			
	D	A	T	A		E	V	E	R	E	S	T		
J	F	K	J	R		B	A	B	U		E	L	L	E
O	R	E	O		M	A	K	E	M	I	N	E	A	X
S	E	R	B		A	L	E	R		M	A	N	N	A
H	E	N	S		E	L	Y	S		F	L	A	G	S

H	E	S		T	H	E	R	E	S			R	B	C
C	A	R		O	A	T	E	R	S		B	O	E	R
P	R	O		O	N	A	P	A	R		O	H	H	I
	S	P	F		E	S	S	E	N	C	E	S		
V	A	S	E		C	R	E	E		K	E	N	A	I
E	R	I	E		O	Y	L		H	O	D	A	D	S
R	I	C	K		C	A	S	B	A	H				
B	A	S	S	O	O	N		U	N	C	A	G	E	D
	G	A	S	H	O	G		O	N	M	E			
E	D	G	A	R	S		O	N	E		R	I	T	E
D	O	N	N	A		P	L	O	D		T	B	S	P
S	P	O	T	C	A	R	D		D	A	M			
E	I	R	E		N	I	S	S	A	N		I	R	S
L	E	T	S		N	A	U	S	E	A		L	H	O
S	R	S		I	M	P	I	S	H		C	O	X	

48   This Puzzle Packs a Wallop

B	I	C		B	C	C			C	O	E	R	C	E
L	S	U		O	U	T		B	U	M	D	E	A	L
D	E	T	E	C	T	S		A	T	I	S	S	U	E
G	E	I	S	E	L		C	H	I	C		E	S	C
		E	L	L	A		U	N	C	R	A	T	E	
I	S	P		L	S	A	T		L	O	U			
T	H	I	S	I	S	I	T		E	N	D	U	R	E
S	U	E	T		S	L	Y	E	R		I	P	O	D
Y	E	S	Y	O	U		S	T	E	N	O	P	A	D
		N	A	P		A	C	M	E		E	R	A	
	I	N	E	R	R	O	R		O	M	A	R		
I	D	A		L	E	A	K		V	E	L	C	R	O
R	E	D	E	E	M	S		R	E	S	C	U	E	D
K	N	E	S	S	E	T		I	R	E		T	A	D
S	T	R	E	S	S			A	S	S		S	R	S

49   Three No Trump?

J	U	N	E	B	U	G		B	L	U	E	L	A	W
U	T	E	R	I	N	E		R	E	S	L	A	T	E
M	I	R	R	O	R	S		A	G	E	S	P	O	T
P	C	T		G	E	T	S	S	O	R	E			
	A	S	H		S	E	I	S	M	S		A	B	S
		O	A	T		D	R	E		C	R	O	W	
S	P	A	T	E		R	E	I	N	F	O	R	C	E
P	E	S	T	O		U	S	N		E	R	I	C	A
A	C	T	I	N	G	B	U	G		E	N	D	I	T
C	A	R	E		R	E	I		U	T	E			
E	N	O		M	I	L	T	O	N		A	S	K	
		L	A	M	B	S	K	I	N		H	U	B	
A	M	R	A	D	I	O		A	T	O	N	E	G	O
P	I	T	C	R	E	W		P	E	D	A	L	E	D
E	A	S	T	E	R	S		I	D	E	A	L	L	Y

```
    P A S H A     F I E F     P J S
R O D M A N     A S E A     R A P
E K E O U T     K I L N     A M O
G E N T L E M E N S ♣     L E O
A D I E U     T I T     R I S K
L A N     P A I D O F F I N ♠ S
    T E E     A D S     L O S E R
    D A N A     F I R E
    N A I A D     J A N     N P R
◇ I N T H E R O U G H     L E N
R A Y S     A N N     I T A L O
I G O     ♡ B R E A K H O T E L
N A N     E R I S     W A V E A T
G R E     N I T E     A T E A S E
S A S     S O Y S     I S S U E
```

```
E T D S     J O J O     P O D S
R O U T     I B E T     I N I T
R U L E     L E F T     E T N A
    G L A D L Y F O R T H E
S H A M U         A R E S O
F I R S T T I M E T O D A Y
O E D     I M N E X T     L T S
        M E C K W E L L
A P S E S         E P P I E
C U E S     B E L A     S L A T
A L A     B R E A C H     A G T
I L L K N O W W H A T Y O U
    E R A S     T I E D
H A V E I N Y O U R H A N D
C L E M     A E O N     E T A T
P I L E     N A N G     E E G S
```

That's an Ugly Split

```
L E S S . P O P S . F L A G .
E C H O . I N R E . R O C H E
D O U B L E T O N . E P C O T
. . S E P I A . U T E R U S
A G O . H A M M A N S R U L E
H O T L I N E . E P A . E S Q
A L T O . . . L O E W S . .
. F O L L O W I N G S U I T .
. . L A P E L . . N O R A
A T O . T E S . G A U G U I N
C O N V E N T I O N S . S O N
C R E E P S . C R U S T . .
T R I L L . B A D B R E A K S
S E L M A . A M O I . A S E A
. S L A Y . T E N S . S A Y C
```

CPSIA information can be obtained
at www.ICGtesting.com
Printed in the USA
BVHW090351141120
593070BV00008B/631